Alexander Medvedkin

KINOfiles Filmmakers' Companions
General Editor: Richard Taylor

Written for cineastes and students alike, and building on the achievements of the KINOfiles Film Companions, the KINOfiles Filmmakers' Companions are readable, authoritative, illustrated companion handbooks to the most important and interesting people who have participated in Russian cinema from its beginnings to the present. Each KINOfile examines the career of one filmmaker, or group of filmmakers, in the context of both Russian and world cinema. KINOfiles also include studies of people who have been active in the cinemas of the other countries that once formed part of the Soviet Union, as well as of émigré filmmakers working in the Russian tradition.

KINOfiles form a part of KINO: The Russian Cinema Series.

Filmmakers' Companions:

Film Companions:

ALEXANDER MEDVEDKIN

EMMA WIDDIS

KINOfiles Filmmakers' Companion 2

I.B. TAURIS

LONDON · NEW YORK

Published in 2005 by I.B.Tauris & Co. Ltd
6 Salem Road, London W2 4BU
175 Fifth Avenue, New York NY 10010
ibtauris.com

In the United States and Canada distributed by Palgrave Macmillan, a
division of St. Martin's Press
175 Fifth Avenue, New York NY 10010

ISBN 1 85043 405 0
EAN 978 1 85043 405 4

A full CIP record for this book is available from the British Library

Typeset in Calisto by Dexter Haven Associates Ltd, London
Printed and bound in Great Britain by
TJ International Ltd, Padstow, Cornwall

Contents

Illustrations

Acknowledgements

Thanks must go to Trinity College for the funding that made the research for this book possible. In Russia, I am extremely grateful to Valerii Bossenko, Nikolai Izvolov and Grigori Borodin, Marina Karaseva, Lena Dolgopiat, Naum Kleiman and all the staff at the Museum of Cinema in Moscow for all their help and support, both intellectual and practical. I also thank the following for their help with procuring materials, and for their sensitive readings of the manuscript in earlier stages: Birgit Beumers, Richard Taylor, Chris Ward and Julian Graffy. Polly McMichael was of invaluable aid, and my friends and family offered crucial moral support. Finally, I owe a huge debt to the whole Polonsky family (Dora included), whose welcome made the experience far more pleasant than by rights it ought to have been.

I dedicate this book to my husband Jason, as a souvenir of the year in which it was finished.

Note on Transliteration

Transliteration from the Cyrillic to the Latin alphabet is a perennial problem for writers on Russian subjects. I have opted for a dual system: in the text I have used the Library of Congress system (without diacritics), but I have broken away from this system (a) when a Russian name has a clear English version (e.g. Maria instead of Mariia, Alexander instead of Aleksandr); (b) when a Russian name has an accepted English spelling, or when Russian names are of Germanic origin (e.g. Meyerhold instead of Meierkhol'd; Eisenstein instead of Eizenshtein); (c) when a Russian name ends in –ii or –yi, this is replaced by a single –y (e.g. Dostoevsky) for a surname and a single –i for a first name (e.g. Grigori, Sergei). In the scholarly apparatus I have adhered to the Library of Congress system (with diacritics) for the specialist.

Introduction

...the gaze of a man who had seen vast spaces, but who – even across them – had not stopped seeing his childhood.[1]

Beginning in Penza in 1900, and ending in Moscow in 1989, the life story of Alexander Ivanovich Medvedkin echoes the story of the Russian Revolution, and of the Soviet dream itself. It is a story of social transformation: of how an uneducated young man was turned into a soldier, thence into a man of culture, and eventually into one of the most respected film-makers of his generation. It is a story of a complex and fluctuating relationship with the political ideals and realities of the age, of a creative life both nurtured and damaged by politics. As such, it is an archetypal story of its time.

The son of a railwayman, of peasant stock, Medvedkin began his career in cinema within the political and cultural ferment of the 1920s. He made his best-known feature films during the Stalin years, and was honoured as a 'People's Artist' of the USSR in 1969, yet he described his creative life as 'driven by the hate, or simply the enmity, of the leadership'.[2] Despite this, he continued to make films and to write screenplays into his final years; he was feted on all his birthdays by the Union of Cinematographers, and he died before the collapse of the state to which he had dedicated his life.

Medvedkin's career, and his life, run in parallel with the life and death of the USSR, and mirror the complexities and moral ambiguities of that ill-fated experiment. His major works stand as testament to the tensions and creativity of the years between 1917 and 1940, at once conforming to the political imperatives of the age and subverting them. His creative life is emblematic of the difficult trajectory of an artist committed to that most capricious of regimes.

There can be little doubt about Medvedkin's ideological commitment to communism – or about his desire to use cinema to serve that end. Nor, however, can there be any doubt about the difficulties that he encountered. As he wrote in 1963, 'If you commit yourself once and for all to the great Soviet Cinema, then you have to find the strength for great argument and profound reflection'.[3] By temperament, Medvedkin was something of a fighter: 'I have never avoided polemic,' he wrote: 'and an absence of creative disagreement in cinema has never seemed to me to be a sign of creativity or well-being.'[4] For him, art could be – indeed, must be – propaganda, an expression of the artist's 'inner commitment to the Party' (*partiinost'*), and 'although this is not, of course, the only path in art, once I had chosen it for myself I tried to be faithful to it to the end'.[5] His creative life was marked by the search for a cinematic form that would meet the demands of that difficult path.

*   *   *

In this book, I attempt to tell the story of that search. This is the first English-language monograph on this most neglected of directors. Although the French director Chris Marker made an extraordinary film, *Le Tombeau d'Alexandre* [*The Last Bolshevik*, 1993], about Medvedkin's life and art, he remains little known. Scholarly research on Medvedkin's work is still in its infancy, in Russia as in the West. There is still only one monograph on the director in Russian, and that was written during the Soviet period.[6] Things are changing, however. A recent issue of the academic cinema journal *Kinovedcheskie zapiski* published a full filmography of the director's works, together with much of his unpublished correspondence with Chris Marker.[7] The film historian Nikolai Izvolov, whose work on the director and his films has been of immense importance, has recently published a chapter on Medvedkin's work in which he raises a number of vital new questions.[8]

For a Western audience, however, Medvedkin's work is still mysterious. Apart from *Happiness* [Schast'e, 1935], few of his films have yet had the impact on the history of world cinema that they perhaps deserve. Even *Happiness* – acclaimed by Sergei Eisenstein as early as 1935 as a classic of Soviet cinema – rarely forms part of the canon of Soviet films familiar to an international audience. This situation is beginning to change. The French–German television channel ARTE has just produced a new print of *Happiness*, and a DVD version of the film is to be released over the next few years.[9] It is to be hoped that Medvedkin's other early feature films – *The Miracle Worker* [Chudesnitsa, 1936] and *New Moscow* [Novaia Moskva, 1938] – may soon find wider exposure.

For pragmatic reasons, therefore, this study of Medvedkin is weighted towards these three early films, the works most likely to be available to my reader. There is another, more significant, reason for this, however. The years between 1920 and 1940 represent the most creatively productive and exciting period of Medvedkin's career. These first films represent the pinnacle of his cinematic achievement. They trace the evolution of his unique dream to create a new kind of political satire, and its frustration.

Medvedkin's first feature films have an important story to tell. They may seem at times to be ambivalent, or even ambiguous, in relation to the dominant ideology of the age. Yet his commitment to the ideals of Bolshevism, and of the Soviet Union, is indisputable. His Party card is preserved in the archive alongside his most cherished papers. And, until his very last days in 1989, he was a celebrated survivor and soldier of the regime that was beginning to disintegrate around him.

Thus, the principal challenge facing any research on Medvedkin lies in the discrepancy between the director's ideological commitment to the regime and the apparent subversiveness of the film texts themselves. For Medvedkin is not an artist who can be conscripted to an anti-Soviet cause. While he may have had a complex and fluctuating relationship with the Soviet regime, he was bred – and remained – a committed Bolshevik. My intent is not to resolve these contradictions. They are, after all, to be found in many such men and women of his time, caught between the political ideals of Bolshevism and its practical manifestation as Soviet communism, faced with the pragmatic and very real imperative of survival at a dangerous time.

Any study of Medvedkin's work has a rich body of resources on which to rely. At the very beginning of his career he began keeping extensive diaries and working notebooks, in which he would record his ideas, keep records of his impressions from films or performances that he had seen, sketch out frame-by-frame plans for future productions, etc. He continued to write such diaries throughout his life, and – with a consciousness of his own historical significance for which we can now be grateful – he preserved the majority of them, and of his notebooks.

This vast archive is now kept in the Moscow Museum of Cinema, providing an invaluable source for the biographer and film historian alike. It is testament, above all, to the director's ongoing quest for a 'new way' of communicating, a new cinematic genre, that occupied his entire life.

For me, then, this study of Medvedkin has two stories to tell. The first is that of a remarkable film-maker. This is a timeless story, told through the analysis of films that stand the test of time. The second is that of a film-maker Revolutionary, and a regime. It is, in a sense, a story of the Soviet century. And it too, I believe, can be told through Medvedkin's films.

There is another narrative on the shelves of that cupboard in the Museum of Cinema, however. And that is the story of a man's sense of personal significance – a man who saw himself through the prism of his age. Medvedkin's absolute confidence in the value of these documents is testament to his confidence in his history as one that mattered. Whether it does – whether Medvedkin's legacy, cinematic or personal, is an important one – is a question that I leave it to the reader to answer.

Curriculum Vitae

1900	Born in Penza, son of a railway worker.
1919	Joined the Red Army as adjutant in Budenny's 'Red Cavalry'.
1921	Moved to the Propaganda Sector of the same cavalry, as head of regimental 'club'.
1922	Moved to Propaganda Division of Western Front.
1925	Promoted to become 'instructor' in the Central (State) Propaganda Division of the Red Army.
1927–1929	Moved to the military film organisation 'Gosvoenkino' and qualified as a film director.
1930–1931	Together with a small working group, Medvedkin made five short experimental, satirical films, which provoked significant debate in the cinematographic community.
1931–1932	Set up and headed the 'film-train,' a travelling film studio that journeyed across the Soviet Union during the First Five-Year Plan.
1933	Became a salaried employee of the central film studio, Mosfilm.

1934	Produced his best-known feature film, *Happiness*.
1935–1936	Began production of *The Accursed Force*, but was forbidden to continue.
1936–1937	Produced *The Miracle Worker*.
1939	*New Moscow* was finished, but was withdrawn from distribution.
1941–1942	Head of film studio in Baku (Azerbaijan), when the making of feature films was evacuated out of the capital during the Second World War.
1943–1945	Worked on the '3rd Belorussian Front' as head of a group of film-makers, recording material at the front line.
1946	Produced an animated feature, *Emergency Service*, which was banned before release.
1954–1958	Worked in Kazakhstan filming Khrushchev's 'Virgin Lands' campaigns for land reclamation. Produced a feature film, *The Liberated Land*.
1959–1989	Produced a series of documentary film 'pamphlets', generally attacking 'international imperialism'.
1968	Met Chris Marker in Leipzig.
1969	Awarded the honour of 'People's Artist of the USSR'.
1970	Premiere of *Happiness* in Paris, organised by Chris Marker.
1977	Premiere of *The Miracle Worker* in Paris.
1979	Awarded the honour of 'People's Artist' for the second time.
1989	Died in Moscow.

1. Political Satire

Medvedkin was only seventeen when the Bolsheviks seized power in Russia. After an education acquired in a Church-run school in his home town of Penza, he had just begun to study in a 'technical college' when the Revolution over-turned his world. His youthful imagination captured, he joined the Red Army in 1919. He served first as a soldier and then as an adjutant in Budenny's famous First Red Cavalry (immortalised by the writer Isaac Babel in his collection of short stories, *Red Cavalry* [1926]), and became a card-carrying member of the Communist Party in 1920.

Medvedkin's excitement at membership of the cavalry, and his sense of the momentousness of the time, is evident in one of his very first diaries, which begins with the underlined heading 'A souvenir: from the First Red Cavalry'.[1] For this ardent enthusiast, Budenny's cavalry was the purest of adventures; as he later explained on film to Chris Marker, 'It was a romantic army...the most fantastical period of my life.'

Military service had other, far-reaching consequences for Medvedkin, however, and the spring of 1920 was the founding moment of his artistic career.[2] Involved in theatre productions for his regimental club, he became preoccupied by the project of education, of using entertainment as 'a means of turning a simple illiterate man into a great soldier'. 'I declared war on verbosity,' he recalled, rejecting written propaganda and seeking alternative forms of communication with the 'ordinary' citizens, workers and peasants, who made up the Red Army during the difficult years of the Civil War.[3]

A Comedy of Attractions

With a comrade, Medvedkin began to produce a new type of theatre performance for his audience of tired and often dispirited peasant-soldiers.
'Somehow, spontaneously,' he recalled, 'we discovered a genre, close to
clowning, inventing comic subjects and dialogues as we went along.'[4] In his
memoirs, these improvised performances emerge as a curious mixture of
techniques and devices, with a long list of influences, including 'buffonade',
'satirical clowning', folklore, operetta and comic turns.[5] This experimental mix
of genres would later provide the artistic basis for Medvedkin's work in cinema.
    The performance he writes of with the greatest affection was an impro-
visation entitled 'A Meeting of Horses'.[6] It had a simple educational message
– that a cavalryman must look after his horse – and was designed to target the
poor treatment of horses by members of Medvedkin's brigade. A kind of
equine general assembly was re-enacted on stage, with all the actors wearing
horse-head masks. The 'horses' complained about their treatment, recounting
how they were ignored while their officers cavorted. Examples of maltreat-
ment abounded: one horse had been beaten, another had been given alcohol
and got drunk, another had been left out in the cold.[7] Real abuses were
described, and particular culprits were named and shamed on stage, as the
horses addressed their complaints directly to members of the audience.
    The performance was, according to the director, 'a very jolly, very impas-
sioned and very caustic method of satire…it worked like a good whip, lashing
whatever harm was done to horses, making it impossible. Everyone was afraid
that they'd be a target.'[8] For Medvedkin, this 'lash' was part of the 'limitless
power of laughter', and he began to be convinced of the vital force of comedy
and satire as weapons in the construction of the ideal Soviet society. His
caricatures and comic sketches were more powerful, he believed, than any
straightforward propaganda message.
    Medvedkin's theatrical achievements were soon recognised by his superiors,
and in 1921 he was moved from active service to work full-time in the Political
Agitation Division of the same regiment, producing educational entertainment. From there, he rose through the ranks of the Red Army's propaganda
machinery, becoming a member of its Central Propaganda Division in 1925.
    As a 'political worker' (*politrabotnik*, a term used to describe those profes-
sional engaged in the practice of propaganda and 'agitation'), Medvedkin
found himself in the thick of politics. And, like any ambitious young man,
he was anxious to make a name for himself in the right circles. In his diaries
from 1924 we find notes taken during a speech given by Mikhail Frunze (who
replaced Leon Trotsky as Commissar for War in 1925), and accounts of
meetings with delegations from the Comintern (the organisation of foreign

communist parties based in Moscow 1919–1943). We can also trace his impassioned relationship with the politics and ideals of the new regime: on 15 July 1924, returning to Moscow from Smolensk, he describes the emotion he felt at his first sight of the wooden mausoleum erected on Red Square to house the recently embalmed body of Vladimir Lenin (who had died in January 1924): 'My heart was bursting. My mind was turbulent. I felt weak.'[9]

As he rose through the ranks of the Red Army's propaganda machine, Medvedkin was exposed to more and more diverse cultural forms, and the young man whose education had been curtailed by the Revolution became a determined autodidact.[10] In a diary entry for 23 September 1928, for example, we find a careful list under the heading 'What I must read about art', which includes Georgi Plekhanov's works on art, and books on the theatre by and about Konstantin Stanislavsky (director of the influential Moscow Arts Theatre, pioneer of theatrical 'naturalism' in Russia) and the avant-garde director Vsevolod Meyerhold.[11] From soldier to man of culture: Medvedkin's journey had begun.

Cinema

In 1927 Medvedkin was affiliated to the State Military Cinema Organisation (Gosvoenkino), and embarked upon the decisive path of his career. The task of Gosvoenkino was twofold: to investigate the potential of cinema as a weapon for propaganda in the event of war; and to produce short films to be shown at army clubs, seeking to educate and encourage young soldiers in the fulfilment of their duty.[12] For Medvedkin, film was a new medium, about which he claimed to have known nothing in 1927. He learned quickly, however, and the move was a fortuitous one: the 'war on verbosity' that he had begun in theatre found its natural expression in silent cinema.[13] Medvedkin had found his art.

Between 1927 and 1929 Medvedkin made six educational films for Gosvoenkino, of which only one has been preserved. Part of broader educational and propaganda campaigns that involved posters and leaflets with simple messages, these films were themselves 'agit-posters' (*agit-plakaty*), seeking maximum clarity and impact. As such they drew their aesthetics and structure from the growing propaganda tradition of the *agitka* – a short film conveying, as Richard Taylor describes it, 'a simple message on a single subject with directness and economy'.[14]

The one surviving filmed 'agit-poster' that Medvedkin produced during this period is entitled *Take Care of your Health* [Beregi zdorov'e, 1929]. It sought to teach the proletarian soldier personal hygiene, to stave off illness and death in the battalions of the Red Army, and used a winning combination of dramatic message and gentle satire. Medvedkin's original sketches for the film, for example, show a striking first frame of a skull in close-up. The camera zooms closer and closer to the skull, with an intertitle – 'Pestilence and a lack of cleanliness have taken thousands of the best fighters from the ranks of the Red Army' – finally superimposed upon its gaping, empty eye sockets. The second sequence shows a two-dimensional silhouette of the army moving across the brow of a hill. Some soldiers fall, leaving a smaller number of silhouettes. Gradually, more and more of them fall, and disappear (Medvedkin using the technical possibilities of a dissolve), so that the army diminishes almost to nothing. In his notes, Medvedkin emphasised the need for this sequence to be 'symbolically' representative, for the movement to be slow and distinct, leaving nothing open to doubt: soldiers' lack of personal hygiene is ravaging the army.[15]

Later in the film, the educational project begins in earnest: we see a soldier learning to wash, and we laugh as he – although appearing burly and tough – reveals himself to be 'afraid' of water. Cross-cutting with shots of a cat, licking her paw to groom herself, Medvedkin shows the soldier timidly attempting to use the shower in the same way, with titles clearly explaining to the spectator what he *should* be doing. Thus the film's message is conveyed through a complex blend of devices, anticipating Medvedkin's later work. It is pared down, given dramatic emphasis, relying initially on techniques of shock and exaggeration, and using images rather than words. Having gained the attention of its target audience, it uses the satirical blend of humour and humiliation, mixing stylisation (the silhouette and the dissolve) with 'real' footage (the man in the shower), to force home the educational message.

Medvedkin's early experience in cinema, then, was part of the mass propaganda effort that began shortly after 1917, and in which film had a key role to play. He was, throughout the 1920s, engaged in the practice and practicalities of propaganda – more an administrator and propaganda officer than he was a film-maker or artist. And he was always keen to avoid the labels of 'art'. For him, artistic experiment was legitimated only by political imperative. From the beginning, however, his work was different from other propaganda film – even from the very best of that genre. From 1918 on, for example, the radical film-maker Dziga Vertov and his 'film-eye' group were engaged in the production of short newsreels (the *Film-Week* [Kinonedelia, from 1918] and *Film Truth* [Kinopravda, from 1923] series), in which the dissemination of the glorious 'truths' of the age was a key imperative. For Medvedkin, film was more than communication, however extraordinary: it was a form of *dialogue*. Using devices perfected in the army theatre, he addressed his spectator directly, encouraging participation and, above all, self-awareness.

Films for the Five-Year Plan

As Stalin's First Five-Year Plan (1928–1933) for agricultural and industrial reconstruction took hold, Medvedkin sought to carry his 'military' cinema forward into the contemporary battle – the struggle for socialist reconstruction. In his memoirs, he recalls the years of the first Plan with nostalgia as an 'unrepeatable hubbub' of 'difficult days and unquiet nights', when the project of making satire work in the service of the state became even more urgent. Cinema in its present form, he felt, was not reflecting the energy and significance of the times: 'When it's a question of the Promfinplan [the Five-Year Plan], of the quality of production, or matters in collective farms – in a word, when it is a question of the fighting parts of the Five-Year Plan, our "great silent" [cinema] does not speak clearly; it stutters, or babbles something inarticulate and always out of place.'[16] He declared war on 'old' cinema (on the popular dramas and American imports that still formed the bulk of Russian movie-going), planning to 'turn it on its head'.[17] In its place, 'an arsenal of new forms of agitational cinema' was needed.

One of Medvedkin's colleagues in Gosvoenkino, Nikolai Okhlopkov, had previously worked as an actor in the experimental theatre of Meyerhold.[18] Together, he and Medvedkin made one educational propaganda film in 1929; in 1930 they embarked upon something quite different: a feature film entitled *The Way of the Enthusiasts* [Put' entuziastov], on which Medvedkin worked as assistant director to the older man. This film, the sketch plans of which remain in Medvedkin's archive, followed the path and adventures of a somewhat sweaty worker through the Civil War.[19] The film was finished, but was then banned before it could be released, and, although obviously disappointed, Medvedkin later claimed to have understood that political decision, acknowledging that 'The film was philosophically confused'.[20] For him, however, its value lay in the experiments and 'creative innovations' that it had enabled, and that he carried forward into future work.

Apparently undaunted, in the autumn of the same year Medvedkin formed a small working group and made three short films, each lasting twelve to fourteen minutes.[21] Responding to calls for industrial 'shock work' and rapid production during the Plan, *Stop Thief* [Derzhi vora], *Poleshko* and *Fruit and Vegetables* [Frukty-ovoshchi] were completed in the extraordinarily short period of two months. They were followed in early 1931 by two films of slightly greater length: *About a White Bull-Calf* [Pro belogo bychka] and *You're Stupid, Mr Stupid* [Duren' ty, duren']. The latter, as a newspaper article proudly declared, was produced in one month, used only 400 metres of film, and cost a mere 7000 roubles.[22]

Such financial economy was echoed in stylistic economy. The films' brevity allowed for nothing 'superfluous' – 'not a single superfluous episode in the screenplay, not a single superfluous frame in an episode, not a single super-fluous object in a frame'.[23] Each was, Medvedkin explained, 'the reworking of a political thesis into the state of a proverb, an aphorism, or a fable' – the attempt to communicate a political truth.[24]

Targeted Satire: the Case of Mr Stupid

Each film attacked a different social ill, a different threat to the success of the Plan. *You're Stupid, Mr Stupid*, for example, addressed the problem of bureaucracy – ever a rich subject in Russian and Soviet culture. Its anti-hero, the eponymous Ivan Ivanovich Duren (the name is derived from 'fool' [*durak*]), seems to achieve ever greater power in the Soviet bureaucracy despite – or perhaps because of – his extreme stupidity. He is an engineer, but one driven by ideas rather than common sense. As the film begins, he inspects a large factory building constructed according to his plans, and discovers that he has made the doors too small to allow any equipment to be installed. Counter-intuitively, instead of merely enlarging the doors he orders the building to be destroyed, in order that the machines can be put inside – inside a building that will, of course, no longer exist.

Medvedkin claimed that *You're Stupid* was based on a familiar Russian folk-tale, about a fool whose behaviour is always misjudged, who dances at funerals and sings funeral songs at a wedding. 'I brought all this up to date,' he claimed, in terms relevant to the Plan.[25] More than just a fool, however, the modern Duren lives by slogans and political rhetoric, lacking the pragmatism essential to the kind of huge-scale transformation demanded by the Five-Year Plan. With his blind adherence to Party dictates, his inability to apply his own intelligence to a given problem, he is, in a sense, a quintessential anti-hero of this confused and chaotic time.

Throughout the film, Duren is marked by his adherence to 'plans' and to paperwork (in several scenes, the screenplay describes him as surrounded by a sea of paper), and his inability to engage with the real problems of con-struction.[26] He exists in a world ruled by documentation, driven by an idealised vision of the socialist Utopia that overrides pragmatism, where 'the idea' dominates over reality. In another episode, later in the film, he orders construction to cease on a site because he cannot find the 'plan', while people in the village are dying from lack of water. The climax of the film arrives as he issues an order for the destruction of an entire village *before* beginning the construction of the new one that is to replace it. All the existing houses are knocked down, and Duren sets about organising a commission to oversee the planning of the new settlement, sorting out paperwork. Meanwhile, the inhabitants gather, forlorn and homeless, in the former town square.

Duren is a bureaucrat par excellence. As such, he is part of a gallery of comic characters that had long been an object of attack in pre-Revolutionary Russian satire. Anton Chekhov's short story of 1888, 'Death of a Bureaucrat', for example, held the intricacies of the pre-Revolutionary bureaucratic hierarchies up to ridicule. In the post-Revolutionary context, however, the situation was more complicated. Certainly, bureaucracy remained; and the state campaign against 'bureaucratism' seemed to offer satiric opportunities.[27] In this respect, Duren is a blend of characters who appear elsewhere in Soviet satire of the period. In 1928, for example, Iakov Protazanov's *Don Diego and Pelageia* had targeted a similarly thoughtless application of principle over pragmatism, with a story of an over-officious village stationmaster. That film was a rare success, however, and the subject of bureaucracy was a sensitive one. The following year, a film by the Georgian director Kote Mikaberidze, entitled *My Grandmother* [Moia babushka, 1929], treating the same problem, was shelved before release. Similarly, Andrei Platonov's novella *The Foundation Pit* (1929), in which the engineer Prushevsky is driven by the desire to create socialism by plan, to build a 'general proletariat home', that will automatically create a new kind of society, was published in the Soviet Union only in 1987.[28] In *You're Stupid, Mr Stupid*, therefore, directing his satire at the thoughtless bureaucracy of a representative of the Soviet state, Medvedkin was treading a dangerous line.

The Problem of Comedy

These early films provoked fervent debate among film practitioners throughout 1930 and 1931. Emerging as they did at a somewhat awkward – and significant – moment in Soviet cultural history, as the relative freedom of the 1920s gave way to the orthodoxies of Stalinism, Medvedkin's films acted as a lens through which a broader debate on the nature of Soviet comedy and satire was focused. What was it appropriate (and permissible) to laugh at in the new Soviet state? What was, or could be, 'Bolshevik comedy', and how could satire serve the young state?

This was a debate that had begun in the 1920s, and involved artists and bureaucrats across a broad spectrum. Indeed, for Medvedkin's project to be successful, it seemed that the very convention of comedy ('eccentric' comedy, or farce) needed to be 'rescued' from its corrupt Western form. The most successful comic films of the time were those of Charlie Chaplin, Buster Keaton and Harold Lloyd: they were widely distributed in Russia, and had significant influence on the evolution of comic techniques there.[29] In Lev Kuleshov's *The Extraordinary Adventures of Mr West in the Land of the Bolsheviks* [Neobychainye prikliucheniia Mistera Vesta v strane bol'shevikov, 1924], for example, we see clear evidence of the techniques of slapstick being appropriated from the Western model. Yet these models were products of an alien ideology, of the much-maligned superficial, destructive environment of US capitalism. Just as the 'foreign' techniques of editing were appropriated and transformed by early Soviet film-makers into the revolutionary techniques of montage, so comedy itself had to be remade according to the new political imperative.

Above all, socialist comedy could not be 'purposeless', could not echo the so-called careless decadence of the American genre. With the serious task of building Utopia on their hands, Soviet workers would have little time for 'mere' entertainment. Yet, if the American form was inappropriate to the Soviet cause, still there was no Soviet or Russian archetype to build on. Pre-Revolutionary Russian cinema had been dominated by melodrama and literary adaptation, and the few early comedies that had been produced (such as Eduard Puchalksy's *Antosha Ruined by a Corset* [Antosha korset pogubil, 1916]) were largely light-hearted and situational. Similarly, comedies of the early 1920s – such as Zheliabuzhsky's *Cigarette Girl from Mosselprom* [Papirosnitsa ot Mosselproma, 1924] and the works of Boris Barnet, among others – lacked the ideological clarity and educational import that was surely appropriate to truly 'Soviet' comedy. What was needed was an entirely new form, quite free from either Western or Russian convention. It was this that Medvedkin set out to provide.

Satire for the State

The problem was not merely one of precedent, however. The difficulties of comedy – and of satire specifically – in the early Soviet period were deep-rooted, and clearly stated in debates held on the pages of the central newspaper, *Literaturnaia gazeta*, in 1929 and 1930. In late 1929 the critic Vladimir Blium described satire as intrinsically destabilising to the social order, seeking to overturn the status quo; any Soviet artist who challenged the existing social order would be acting as a counter-Revolutionary.[30] Historically the weapon of the oppressed classes, satire appeared impossible and unnecessary in the new political order. The Soviet proletariat was no longer oppressed: it was celebrated as a 'dictator' in a supposedly classless society, and as such had no need for satire. At the same time, 'purposeless' comedy had no meaning for the working class, for whom, according to the literary critic Nusinov, a sense of humour was 'alien'.[31]

There were many, however, who saw satire as a means of social improvement that remained essential in the new order. For Medvedkin himself, humour was the strength of the proletariat, the essence of its Revolutionary and subversive spirit, and could be harnessed as a means of social education. For the poet Vladimir Maiakovsky, similarly, satire was a 'weapon in our struggle', and had to be mobilised as such.[32] Its task was to target those who failed to live up to the promise of the Revolution, and to shame them into self-improvement. In the words of the nineteenth-century critic Vissarion Belinsky, 'in opening society's eyes to itself, and being instrumental in awakening its self-consciousness', satire could 'cover vice with scorn and disgrace'.[33]

In the supposedly ideal world of the Soviet Utopia, however, could any vice or problem be acknowledged? The answer to this question took different forms over the first two decades of Soviet power. During the years of the New Economic Policy (NEP; 1921–1928), when the relaxation of strictures regarding petty trade created a curiously hybrid society, and allowed for the revival of the 'petty bourgeois' habits that had been outlawed during the difficult years of War Communism, such satire had an obvious focus. For the ordinary citizen, this time was a curious amalgam: a confusing mix of the political rhetoric of communism and a lived experience of compromise. Many literary and cinematic comedies (such as the 'everyday' film comedies of Barnet and Friedrich Ermler) captured its ideological complexities in word and image.[34] For Maiakovsky, satire was a weapon with which to do battle with the 'petty-bourgeois philistinism' (meshchanstvo), which he found distressingly evident during the messy NEP years. His 1929 play The Bedbug, for example, targeted the grotesque former worker Prisypkin, who changed his name to Pierre Skrypkin, abandoned his proletariat lover Zoia for an aspirational hairdresser, and wanted his home to be a 'cornucopia' of plenty. In similar ways, Abram Room's Bed and Sofa [Tret'ia meshchanskaia, 1929] ostensibly mocked its heroine Liudmila's love of domestic comfort, and charted her path to a more purified social consciousness via the rejection of the comforts of domestic space.[35]

Meshchanstvo, then, was a relatively safe target in the mid-1920s, and could be satirised as a threat to the Revolutionary project without threatening the integrity of the project itself. Medvedkin, however, began making his films during the First Five-Year Plan, in a quite different political climate. The first Plan, initiated in 1928, signalled an emphatic end to the relative tolerance of the NEP period, with the state and people theoretically united behind the banner of socialist reconstruction.

Henceforward, the full grandeur of the Revolutionary project was to be heralded: there was little apparent space for dissent, and the role of satire was once again under threat. In the nascent socialist Utopia, could anything be ridiculed? Maiakovsky's second satirical play, The Bathhouse, was withdrawn from the stage after its first performances in 1930; the poet committed suicide shortly afterwards. And it was at this very moment that Medvedkin set out to use comedy as a corrective, as an aid in the great project of socialist reconstruction, 'to provoke in the spectator not laughter, but a feeling of anger and shame'.[36] His timing was awkward, to say the least.

'Medvedkino': The Debate

In the political climate of 1930–1931 Medvedkin's short satirical films were perplexing and difficult in two respects. First, and perhaps most significantly, they were satirical at a time when satire was dangerous. Second, they were stylistically unusual, and seemed to have no precedent in previous Soviet comedy. They provoked long and awkward discussion among the cinematic and cultural bureaucracy. There are records of at least two major meetings at which Medvedkin's films were officially considered, and the stakes were high: would Medvedkin continue to work in cinema at all?[37]

At the first meeting, after fierce debate, a group of functionaries, actors and film-makers, including Room (director of *Bed and Sofa*), finally resolved to allow the films to be shown to the public, and to permit Medvedkin to continue his work. At the second, a meeting of the Film Production Section of Soiuzkino, Anatoli Lunacharsky was present and spoke at some length. In general, there was a significant voice in favour of Medvedkin's educational ambition and his stylistic innovation at both meetings. The results, however (the films themselves) were universally considered unsuccessful. At best, they hovered uncomfortably between the 'real' and 'caricature'; the clarity of their message was obscured by formal 'experiment'.[38] At worst, with their direct and satirical focus on recognisable Soviet reality, they risked destabilising the Soviet project itself.

In July 1931 the industry newspaper *Kino* dedicated an entire page to discussion of Medvedkin's films.[39] The tone of these published essays took its lead from Anatoli Lunacharsky. Lunacharsky had spoken in muted support of Medvedkin, saying that his search for a viable form of film satire was a valuable one, but that the films themselves were unsuccessful. The problem, he said, was one of focus: satire had to define its target firmly, aiming at the particular rather than the general. It should beware of appearing to indicate too widespread a problem. Medvedkin's vision of the corrupt bureaucrat – Mr Stupid – might suggest, for example, that *all* Soviet bureaucrats were similarly corrupt, and thus threaten the integrity of the process of socialist construction.

Thus, any satire on contemporary Soviet society had to make it clear that its targets were localised, and not endemic: 'We are dealing with a healthy organism, in which there are individual defects, individual survivals of the old, not quite dead, society.'[40] Echoing Lunacharsky, another critic wrote that satire needed 'to be treated with extreme delicacy, or it risks turning into a distorting mirror'.[41] The representation of Soviet reality in this distorted mirror would play into the hands of the 'class enemy', providing them with ammunition: such films were a 'charge, which could turn against us'.[42]

At the root of the objections to satire, then, lay a basic insecurity, a sense of a fragile society under attack. For all this, however, Lunacharsky did believe that there was a place for healthy self-criticism in Soviet cinema. In a later speech, published in the journal *Proletarskoe kino*, he made a firm statement in support of Medvedkin, saying unambiguously: 'We would be terrible masters if we were to knock such an original artist from this great, broad path [...] If we punish every pioneer for his errors, then everyone will be afraid of originality – and that is the end of creativity.'[43]

Medvedkin would later claim that it was only this public support from the influential Lunacharsky that enabled him to continue to work.[44] In fact, it seems that Lunacharsky's may have been the most powerful, but was not the only support that Medvedkin received. In an undated document of 'Resolutions' produced after a screening of *Fruit and Vegetables*, *Stop Thief* and *Poleshko*, the 'Association of Workers in Revolutionary Cinematography' (ARRK; one of the most influential groups of film-makers during this period) made a clear declaration of the importance of satire – both for Soviet cinema and for Soviet society.[45] ARRK called for improved distribution of Medvedkin's work, in order to provide an example to other directors working in the genre. It bemoaned the absence of other comic screenplays for cinema, and emphasised that the development of the short comic film as a genre was a key to the future success of film propaganda.

A New Form

The problem with Medvedkin's films, however, was not just political. Their uniqueness lay in their formal innovation, in their unusually caricatural, pared-down style. In a published article, Medvedkin, who was present at many of the discussions of the films, issued a vociferous defence of his work – an unambiguous statement of his desire to use film comedy as a means of social improvement. Though he acknowledged that his creative method was still only in its infancy, he declared that the future of Soviet cinema lay in precisely the kind of short films that he had begun to produce: the satirical 'poster', the comedy, or the animated caricature.[46]

Critics were united in recognising that Medvedkin was searching for a new direction in film comedy – even if that search was not yet considered successful. He was, according to one critic, seeking a new style, 'a cinematic folk tale or fable'.[47] According to the influential Vladimir Sutyrin, Medvedkin's curious aesthetics were motivated not by a desire for mere 'formalist experiment' (this at a time when 'formalist' directors, such as Sergei Eisenstein, were criticised for prioritising stylistic innovation over political message)[48] but by political imperative.[49]

Medvedkin acknowledged that the films' principal formal device was that of exaggeration, and argued that a certain lack of verisimilitude was inevitable – even desirable. The brevity of the films demanded a single idea, and a film's sole purpose was to convey that idea as clearly as possible, by whatever means. The mimetic or representational ambitions of the work were secondary to its communicative impulse, its message. In his search for a means of conveying this message, Medvedkin drew directly on folkloric techniques of stylisation and exaggeration. Thus he carried into cinema methods that he had first explored in his regimental theatre, where the quest for new forms of entertainment and education had led him to popular culture. Russian folklore, he had discovered, was a rich source of familiar images and narratives through which to communicate with his audience of uneducated soldiers.[50] Its techniques, moreover (simple narratives with a clear message, often conveyed through exaggeration, masks and caricature), seemed ideal for his purposes.

Influences

Of course, this turn to older forms of popular culture in the quest for an specifically Soviet aesthetic was not unique to Medvedkin. In the 1920s Maiakovsky composed verses and images for the State Telegraph Agency (ROSTA) window advertising campaigns. These single-page bulletins, often illustrated comic narratives, drew on the techniques of folk art – and, in particular, of the illustrated woodcut, the *lubok* (see Chapter 3). They were placed in windows, in railway stations and at the front during the Civil War, offering grotesque caricatures of capitalist figures and simple ditties in support of Soviet power.[51] Medvedkin's single-reel features, which drew directly on the simplified aesthetics of the *lubok*, seem to owe much to the ROSTA tradition.

Medvedkin's influences were diverse. In particular, working with Okhlopkov at Gosvoenkino, he had direct access to the techniques and innovations of Vsevolod Meyerhold. Meyerhold (like Medvedkin, a committed Bolshevik), who staged Maiakovsky's satires *The Bedbug* and *The Bathhouse* (1930), as well as his early celebration of the Revolution, *Mystery-Buff* (1918), saw the theatre as a space of communicative interaction between performance and spectator – a mass arena very different from the elite space of the imperial theatre. Like Medvedkin – indeed, like most artists and writers who sought to address their work to the new audience of workers and peasants – he sought alternative ways for theatre to communicate. Rejecting the mimetic drive of Konstantin

Stanislavsky's 'naturalist' experiments in the Moscow Arts Theatre and looking back at ancient theatrical models such as the Italian *commedia dell'arte* and Russian fairground and puppet shows for inspiration, he called for theatre as a self-conscious art of 'stylisation' and theatricality.

It seems likely that Meyerhold's ideas fed directly into Medvedkin's own experiments. In *The Way of the Enthusiasts*, he and Okhlopkov attempted to use a self-conscious interface with the audience as a satiric device: in the opening frames of the screenplay, the worker addresses the camera directly with the words: 'So, what are you fools looking at?' Through Okhlopkov, moreover, Medvedkin began to work with two former members of Meyerhold's troupe, Vladimir Maslatsov and Nikolai Sibiriak, both of whom had been subjected to the rigorous training in the art of clowning and circus skills that the master demanded. Consummate comics, they played the leading roles in all of Medvedkin's short films.[52]

The influence of Meyerhold's theatrical experiments on Soviet cinema more broadly is well documented. Eisenstein, for example, worked closely with the director, and his seminal early essay 'The Montage of Attractions' owes much to early Revolutionary theatre.[53] Indeed, it is productive to view Medvedkin's work within the broader context of early avant-garde aesthetics: the work of Meyerhold, certainly, and also of the group of Petrograd artists who called themselves the Factory of the Eccentric Actor (FEKS), under the leadership of Grigori Kozintsev and Leonid Trauberg, whose energetic experiments re-envisaged cinema and theatre as a series of 'attractions' (the term was much used in this period to describe 'turns' or 'gags', episodically arranged, which replaced the traditionally linear plot of a film or performance).

Eisenstein's theory of the 'montage of attractions' in theatre, and the Eccentrics' experiments in cinema and theatre alike, both drew on the circus as an inspiration, seeking to exploit techniques of 'shock' from practises such as clowning. Medvedkin, too, explicitly stated his interest in adapting the techniques of clowning to his films, exploring the potential of slapstick comedy in educational cinema. And it is this desire to exploit the techniques of 'attractions' to political ends that links him most clearly with his cinematic predecessors in the 1920s.

In Medvedkin's case, however, it was the comic impact of 'attractions' and clowning that was most important. And for that he had other important precedents and examples. His earliest discovery of the power of comedy had been made in the regimental theatre, where he began, he recalled, to use comic devices to move his audience from one 'level' of laughter to another, 'from laughter – to laughter'.[54] He claimed to have had no exposure to American comic cinema before 1930, and that his early experiments with comedy in the soldiers' club were 'entirely original'.[55] For that reason, his 'discovery' of Harold Lloyd (which, according to Medvedkin, took place only in 1930) and of the American comic genre more generally was something of a revelation for him, and he revelled in the apparent 'coincidence' between their working methods and his own.

After seeing Lloyd's *Grandma's Boy* for the first time, Medvedkin later recalled that he spent four days writing out the entire script of the film from memory, frame by frame, with a full analysis of its comic devices. He then returned to view the film for a second time, when, for him, the film's secret was revealed: 'one comic sequence ends and straightaway, without a break, you start to laugh at another gag'.[56] After Lloyd came Chaplin, and Medvedkin discovered the same technique to an even greater extent in Chaplin's early films, which he cites as the most significant influence on his own work.

> A pie is thrown in someone's face and they laugh: Chaplin doesn't let the audience cool down, he disturbs their equanimity. The audience is wound up because it knows that now it will be kicked and it knows that the door will now open and the wife will burst in. Laughter, laughter, laughter. A cascade of laughter, a cascade of funny turns, clown-like turns that are close to the circus. That's the art, the great art, of Chaplin.[57]

This 'layering' of comedy, moving the audience relentlessly forward, propelling them between 'levels' of laughter, was, for Medvedkin, the secret to great comedy, and it was this that he wished to exploit to political ends. Within this, however, he was aware that his 'laughter' was of a different order. His task was one of education, rather than entertainment. 'The satiric path that we have chosen is extremely difficult and thankless. I am often criticised for the fact that our comedies are not funny. But we come to the work from the position that satire need not necessarily inspire laughter.'[58] The humour of the films should, he suggested, inspire 'not a thoughtless chuckle, but an intelligent smile, rich in content'. Levels of laughter would, in his comedy, become levels of consciousness.

It was this search for a balance between laughter and education – the attempt, perhaps, to rein in his comic imagination, to give it ideological weight – that would define Medvedkin's future work. First and foremost, it would define the evolution of his cinematic 'form', his unique poetics. The roots of those poetics were already evident, however. The blend of contemporary themes with the images and devices of traditional Russian folk culture, characteristic of Medvedkin's most interesting work, was already present in these first experiments. Secondly, in these early films we anticipate Medvedkin's rejection of classical narrative and his emphasis on clarity of communication. The early years as a propagandist, in the cradle of the Red Army, offered a combination of experiences and preoccupations that inflect Medvedkin's later films, and help us to understand not only his cinema but also his place in his society.

Most importantly, they mark him as a self-styled man of politics rather than art. From his early work in the military theatre to his cinematic training under the auspices of Gosvoenkino, Medvedkin was closely involved in the practical administrative, financial and organisational aspects of cinema. And it was this intention that underpinned his formal 'experiments'. During the decade that saw Kuleshov's discovery of montage, Eisenstein's theorisation of the montage of 'attractions' and 'intellectual montage' and Vertov's radicalism, Medvedkin cuts a rather strange figure, at once profoundly experimental and profoundly pragmatic. This curious combination of qualities, infused with the director's characteristic energy and fervour, marks all his work.

2. The Film-Train

In Medvedkin's diaries from the late 1920s we find a young man who is pre-occupied with communication in all its forms. His tiny handwriting covers the small pages of successive notebooks with notes on films he has seen, sketches and screenplays. It is in this perpetual and urgent quest for new forms of cinematic communication that the value of Medvedkin's cinematic legacy lies. And it was at its most urgent during the heady years of the First Five-Year Plan, when, in Medvedkin's words, 'the enemy, hiding in our ranks, fought desperately'.[1] His early satire experiments not having proved an unqualified success, Medvedkin must have felt that his desire to serve the Plan – to create a fully politically active cinema – was frustrated. Convinced of the potential of his craft, he sought an alternative project. And he returned, eventually, to an idea that he had first mooted as early as 1930, and one that was to become a myth of cinema history, perhaps his most significant contribution to world cinema: the film-train.[2]

Medvedkin, son of a railwayman, turned to what he knew. The idea was at once simple and absurdly ambitious: the construction of an entire film studio in a train that could travel across the vast expanses of the Soviet Union, using film as a means not only of recording but also of encouraging the realisation of the Five-Year Plan. Medvedkin envisaged film as a direct participant in the construction of the new regime: 'cinema can be not only a weapon "in general",' he wrote, 'but a very real weapon in the Party cells, in concrete areas of socialist construction.'[3] The train would travel across the territory, would film communities – collective farms or provincial factories – in their everyday activities, and then process and show the films immediately, together with ready-made captions such as 'Comrades, this cannot go on...' It aimed to encourage better work practices and thereby to aid the fulfilment of the Plan's targets. In Medvedkin's words, the train would be 'a kind of special fire brigade to put out problem fires' – and to put them out with that most effective of extinguishers: film.[4]

*   *   *

In 1931 the main administrative body for cinema, Soiuzkino, of which Medvedkin was a salaried employee, rejected the idea of the train as impracticable. The young director was not deterred, however, and he eventually secured the support of the Central Committee of the Communist Party – and in particular of the influential Sergo Ordzhonikidze, then Minister of Heavy Industry. This was cinema literally 'in the service of the state'. The train was directly financed by the political, rather than the cinematographic, administration during its first year of operation in 1932, and subject to the command of the Propaganda Section of the Party.

This political affiliation was a source of great pride for Medvedkin. He was keen to stress the team's role as servants – or soldiers – of the Five-Year Plan, 'ordered' to go to a particular place, or 'thrust' into a particular mission – 'a telegram from Moscow required us to rush off to Ukraine'.[5] The train was to be a direct participant in the lives of the communities it visited, agitator and communicator at once. And the cinematic experiments that Medvedkin carried out during the year that he spent 'on wheels' were to shape his later attempts to create political satire.

Practicalities

Three decommissioned train carriages were given to Medvedkin, to be remodelled as the film-train.[6] The finished version contained thirty-two sleeping places (each a single square metre, with comfort not high on Medvedkin's list of priorities), basic food preparation facilities, a film laboratory, an editing suite (six tables), basic animation facilities and a small cinema, with seats and a simple portable projector. Five or six 'crews' (each comprising a director and a cameraman) worked on the train at any one time, each with its own equipment.

Medvedkin's team of thirty-two was made up almost exclusively of young men with little or no experience in cinema. The most active members of the train team during his year of leadership were Karmazinsky, Piotrovsky, Maslennikov, Vladimirov, Bogorov, Lifshits, Bubrik, Afonin and the two actors, Sibiriak and Maslatsov.[7] Only Medvedkin and Nikolai Karmazinsky were relatively experienced directors: Karmazinsky had been working in cinema since 1925, and Medvedkin since 1927.[8]

The young 'romantics' (Medvedkin's description) who joined him on the train had to agree to stringent conditions: that single square metre of sleeping space, unrestricted working hours and an obligation to take part in all areas of film production (with regular examinations as to their capability).[9] Although Medvedkin's daughter, Chongara, claimed (on film to Chris Marker) that she and her mother, Vera, accompanied her father on the train, it is difficult to imagine that their family life was an easy one! Medvedkin's diaries, kept during much of the first year, emphasise the strict regime of the train. During its first year, the train undertook six major journeys, comprising a total of '294 days on wheels', as Medvedkin was later to describe it. It travelled to Dnepropetrovsk in Ukraine, to the Krivoi Rog mining area, to the collective farms in the Crimea, to the Donbass mining region and to the Voronezh region, and produced no fewer than seventy-two films (a total of ninety-one reels, or 24,965 metres of film).

Forty-five years later, from the perspective of 1977, Medvedkin laid stress on the round-the-clock work that his team undertook. Eighteen-hour days were a minimum: 'If someone came to us who was rather indifferent,' he recalls, 'he didn't survive for long if he was idle, if he didn't like getting up in the middle of the night. We'd warn him once, twice, and then quietly, all smiles and without scolding him, we'd buy him a ticket to Moscow.'[10] With its outrageous production timetables the train was a kind of cinematic 'Stakhanovite' (shock worker; those workers praised for 'overfulfilment' of production targets were called 'Stakhanovites' after Alexei Stakhanov, the miner whose record-breaking labour performance sparked hundreds of imitators). The entire team would be mobilised to ensure the fastest possible production of a film ('We film it today and show it tomorrow!' went the catchphrase); on the first trip, one film was produced in a mere eight hours. The work ethos reached an apogee in October 1932, when films of the opening of the Dnieper power station were produced and viewed on the same day by workers in the local area, and sent to Moscow, Kharkov, Kiev and Stalino (Donetsk) within twenty-four hours.

Investigation

The first expedition, in early 1932, was a trip to the Ukrainian mining region of Dnepropetrovsk. Its purpose was to improve the efficiency of industrial transportation systems, to tackle the problems of poor organisation in the factories responsible for servicing railway engines etc. The trip lasted three months, produced nine films, and 'served' 35,300 viewers with 105 screenings.

The principal genre of film used during the first trip was that of the 'film-newspaper' (*kino-gazeta*), and the films produced were, according to Medvedkin, of poor quality. The only surviving film was directed by Karmazinsky, entitled simply *Newspaper no. 4* [Gazeta no. 4] and was one of a series of such filmed newspapers. This very simple reel demonstrates one key aspect of the train's work: the desire to encourage shame. In it, poor workers were named and shamed outright, and local leaders (Medvedkin's favourite target, bureaucracy) were filmed at a lengthy and ill-focused meeting, ignoring the urgent demands of the work that surround them.

Although such 'film-newspapers' might appear to resemble the many other film-newspapers of the time, Medvedkin was at pains to emphasise how different they were. Unlike that of the other film journals, which disseminated images across the Soviet space, the intended audience of these films was not national but local. In Medvedkin's words: 'The principal difference between the film-train and other film factories is that the production of a film is organically and intrinsically linked to its screening in the place of production.'[11] In parallel, the focus of agitation was local; the film-train sought to intervene directly in the life of the communities it visited.

Two days after their return from Dnepropetrovsk the team set off on their second expedition – heading south again, but this time to the Krivoi Rog mining region, to improve the unloading of mined coal. For this trip, Medvedkin produced a plan that aimed to expand the train's remit into broader agitational work, creating 'brigades' among the workers in every mine, responsible for disseminating the Party message and improving production. Collaborative work with local newspapers would be set up as soon as possible after arrival, and was, Medvedkin believed, essential to the success of the project; newspapers and pamphlets could encourage members of the community to attend screenings and to participate in the activities of the train.[12]

Such detailed plans were not wasted: the achievements of this second expedition were substantial. In two months the train produced twenty-one films (more than twice as many as had been made on the first expedition), worked closely with local newspapers and involved a far greater number of workers. Film was no more important than any other medium: 'Anything that was difficult to capture on film we would hit with print, and, in a situation where pamphlets were already proving useless, the combined editorial team tackled the material on screen.'[13] By the end of the second trip the train had begun to create its role as multi-levelled agitator; its cinematic 'shock' was a many-pronged attack that, in the communities it visited, left few stones uncovered, few individuals untouched.

Communication

In some ways, the train project was a response to the difficulties that Medvedkin had encountered with his early satiric shorts. It offered him an opportunity to demonstrate his commitment as 'soldier' of the Five-Year Plan, and to continue and develop the direct propaganda work that he had begun with Gosvoenkino. Yet he did not abandon his longer-term ambition to develop a new genre of political satire, nor did he abandon comedy as a filmic device. Working in the army theatre, Medvedkin had discovered two key techniques as essential in his project of communication: the importance of direct address to the audience, and the value of the comic.

The first of these was immediately put to work on the train, as Medvedkin experimented with further techniques of audience engagement. When describing the films in retrospect, he repeatedly uses the phrase 'the screen asked'. Film was a form of active intervention, a collaborative project with the audience. Medvedkin and his team developed new types of film, appropriate to the needs of the train – and of the time. There was, he claimed, no precedent, no existing film language that they could use. New genres such as the 'socialist reckoning', 'film reports' and 'film-letters' were used to document and criticise the everyday life in the communities visited. Other genres included the 'film-appeal', which involved the participation of a hard-working member of the community in question, who would demonstrate his or her superior labour performance, and encourage other members of the village, factory or farm to follow that example. All these genres, Medvedkin claimed, were 'reports' – not art, but business.[14]

For Medvedkin, the most important films produced by the train were the longer 'film reports', which would tackle a single, particularly urgent problem in a given community. In stark contrast to other genres, these reports could take between ten and fifteen days to produce. One such film, much praised by Medvedkin, was *How's Life, Comrade Miner?* [Kak zhivesh', tovarishch gorniak?], which addressed the problems of living conditions in the October Mine in the Krivoi Rog region – a mine that, according to Medvedkin, was so improved by the experience of the film-train that it subsequently became the most successful mine in the region.[15] This film, directed by Karmazinsky, shows how the camera became a close observer and judge of the daily rituals of the community in question, uncovering the roots of poor organisation in the mine.

The film opens with the mine committee, which has met to discuss problems of low production and work discipline. The meeting is shot, as was frequently the case in the film-train productions, in what approximates to real time, with minimal use of montage. As such, the protracted inefficiency of the committee is revealed, underlined by a focus on the accumulating pile of minutes and documents, which are – markedly – irrelevant to the facts of life in the mine that Karmazinsky sought to reveal. With a satirical reminder of the relentless mockery of bureaucracy in *You're Stupid, Mr Stupid*, as things disintegrate around the mine officials, and papers are in total disarray, an intertitle proclaims ironically that 'The committee meets...' Meanwhile, another title demands: 'What's *your* life like, Comrade Miner?', and the camera proceeds to explore the everyday life of the miners themselves. The answer, we discover, is not a happy one. The film juxtaposes the reality of living conditions with the ideals of Soviet construction, revealing the truth behind state rhetoric. 'There's no obvious "culture officer" in the hostels,' it remarks ironically, demonstrating the failure of state ideals to spread 'culture' and 'civilised behaviour' (*kul'turnost'*) across all sections of the population. Forlorn trees mark the failure to meet the state's suggestion that 'greenery' should embellish living quarters – an ironic jibe at much-publicised 'socialist' intentions to create a Utopian space of leisure for the new prole- tariat. Beds have no mattresses, and no one eats in the communal dining hall. Thirty families live in the space to which the camera follows one miner, the hard-working Ivan.

In simple terms, this film criticised poor standards of living. As such, as Marker points out, it is a uniquely unvarnished document of real life, in stark contrast to the idealised images of Soviet industry that were disseminated for propaganda purposes. Aiming their films at local use, the film-train workers had no qualms about showing the real problems faced by Soviet citizens during the First Plan, and this film is marked, above all, by a tangible sense of sympathy and understanding for 'comrade miner' and his friends. It demonstrates the resilience of the ordinary man and woman, their ability to appropriate and create a habitable space within all this dirt and difficulty: the making of 'home'. With the white residential building continually in the background, it shows how the miners and their families use the space of the mine to create a bearable life. The community prepares meals in the dirt yard in front of the hostel, children play in those forlorn 'green spaces'. Families are crowded together, a young couple seek privacy in a cramped public space. A man sits in an open latrine cubicle while other members of the community walk past. Close-ups show feet struggling on rutted mud paths, emphasising the difficult material conditions of everyday life.

In this film, the camera – intimate and even intrusive – intervened directly in everyday life. Never hidden or anonymous, it was clearly a self-conscious presence in the communities it visited. Its task was a serious one: to reveal the problems of Soviet reality, and to solve them. In the contemporary climate, this was a risky business.

Not everything was serious, however, and Medvedkin had not forgotten the lessons he learned in the army theatre. In addition to such 'reports' and 'reckonings', he recalls comedies produced by the train, which he describes as 'compensating for the lack of entertainment in the "productive" work of the train'.[16] These films aimed to raise awareness of a particular political problem, but in a more diverting way than the serious tone of the other films.

Here, then, we see traces of Medvedkin's former project and principal ambition: the creation of agitational satire. Vladimir Maslatsov, who had starred in the early satires that had caused Medvedkin so much trouble in 1931, was a member of the film-train, and acted in the first 'sharp' comedy that Medvedkin produced on the train, *About Love* [1931], and in a number of others.[17] It was not until the train's third expedition (around the Crimean agricultural regions, observing the work of collective farms on a journey from Evpatoria to Zinov'evsk at harvest time), however, that Medvedkin made the comedy that he considered to be the most successful film made on the train: *Tit*. The eponymous hero of the film, Tit (played by Maslatsov), is in many ways a prototype of the Khmyr, hero of the 1935 comedy *Happiness*. He is an 'Ivan the Fool' (*Ivan-durak*) figure, familiar from Russian folklore, whose good-hearted stupidity is both his downfall and his salvation.[18] In Medvedkin's rhymed intertitle, 'Tit is called Tit because he holds things up' (*Tit, potomu chto Tit, chto delo tormozit*).[19] This film has not been preserved, but the archive does contain a detailed frame-by-frame screenplay, hand-drawn by Medvedkin, through which we can imaginatively reconstruct the plot and devices of the film, following Tit as he gets into a series of scrapes that draw clearly on folk-loric paradigms.[20]

Intervention

Medvedkin described this 'Collective Farm Expedition' of July–August 1932 as the most 'productive' of the year: its eleven films were viewed by some 40,000 people, and a large number of meetings, conferences, etc. were organised over the six-week period. Medvedkin recorded that ten 'kulaks' (a term, which became one of abuse during collectivisation, describing richer peasants who were perceived to be working against the collective good) were 'excluded from the collective farm' during discussions after screenings. As a result of the work of the train, Medvedkin claimed proudly, five collective farms fulfilled the Plan's targets for grain yield. His team were not just observers, moreover: the official statistics from the train also boasted of harvesting 16,380 kilos of wheat in one farm, suggesting a particularly hands-on form of intervention.

During this trip, the team sought to organise 'socialist competition' and local 'rallies' between neighbouring communities – part of a broader state

campaign during the First Five-Year Plan, rewarding individuals and communities for the fulfilment of quotas. Due to the train's activities, twenty-one
collective farms joined the 'All-Soviet' competition for grain yield. In one
agricultural film, *The Veitlus Collective Farm* [Kolkhoz Veitlus], produced
during this trip, we see 'socialist competition in action', with the one collective
farm held up as an example of good production discipline. In contrast, *Yes,
A Chain* [Da, zveno] showed poor harvest methods and lack of incentive,
focusing on the necessity for teamwork and the problems of poor work
discipline. Used together, these films fulfilled Medvedkin's basic strategy of
setting good example against bad: as he wrote in his diary of 1932, 'we must
convey the example of the best to those that are behind'.[21] This idea of competition was central to the train's success.

The last of the train's expeditions under Medvedkin's leadership was to
the Donbass region. It lasted three months, and focused on two distinct areas
of production, coal and steel, aiming to improve Party organisation. This trip
represented, in a sense, the fullest realisation of Medvedkin's ambitions for
the train, and the broadest reach of its agitational remit. During this trip the
team began to produce their own newspaper, *Temp*, turning half of one of their
carriages into a printing press. This also enabled the production of brochures
to accompany educational films, such as *The Blast Furnace* [Domna], part of
a series of animated shorts dedicated to explaining the function of various
pieces of machinery. Such films were produced on lengths of two metres that
were glued together to form a circle, enabling the continuous replay of the
films over periods of up to one hour, thus ensuring that the educational
message could not be ignored. They were produced in vast quantities; three
hundred copies of each, together with accompanying brochures, would enable
them, Medvedkin said, to be in constant use in schools, training centres,
mines, etc.[22]

Participation

The films produced by the train were envisaged as weapons, their principal
purpose being the encouragement of debate. Here, Medvedkin's vision of
film as dialogue found its fullest realisation; he recalls proudly how 'heated
arguments' would spring up after screenings.[23] Taking advantage of the mobility
of their projection facilities, Medvedkin's team organised smaller-scale
screenings, 'in hostels, waiting rooms, in outdoor camps, etc'.[24] The ideal
screening would be to seventy and one hundred people, in their workplace:
in these conditions, the shared experience of the audience and their limited
numbers would facilitate the organisation of targeted discussions; the problems
revealed could be addressed, and resolutions made as to how to remedy them.

Medvedkin believed firmly that film was a more effective means of communicating with the worker or peasant than any verbal medium. In one of his essays about the train, he cites a worker from the Krivbass region: 'What orator could have told us so clearly about the outrages appearing beneath our very eyes? [...] and it didn't just tell us about them, but also made us want to rectify all these problems immediately.'[25] The power of film lay in its impact, its immediacy. It offered the unsuspecting miner, or farmer, a unique experience: that of seeing oneself on screen. And it was in this, perhaps, that the secret of the train's success lay: 'To see on screen one's own friends, one's factory floor, one's own street – that's interesting for anyone,' Medvedkin affirmed.[26] Many of his accounts of viewers' reactions to the films emphasised the shock of self-identification on screen.[27]

According to Izvolov, '[the film-train team] was the first to realise that the screen is not a mirror, but a transformer of life'.[28] It would seem more appropriate, however, to suggest that Medvedkin's team were remarkable for their exploitation and expansion of the potential of the screen precisely *as* a mirror – reflecting to the spectator his or her own life, in all its unsavoury reality. The film-train productions *represented communities to themselves*, granting the local space the symbolic weight of representation. Cinema, after all, was still a relatively new medium, a 'magic mirror', and one that carried a certain mysterious glamour. To see oneself captured within this magic mirror must have been both exciting and disturbing, a process of de-familiarisation that would enable a new kind of awareness of both self and community. For Medvedkin, this process was primarily agitational in purpose, a kind of *interpellation*, through which the politically unconscious man or woman would be transformed into a Soviet citizen, inscribed into the new symbolic order via the camera.

A deep-rooted belief in the ideological weight of *participation* underlay the philosophy of the film-train. Collaboration was a key feature of its work, part of the overall project of team building that underpinned Medvedkin's vision. Members of the local community were involved in the production of the films in various ways – helping to make intertitles etc.[29] As the techniques and processes developed over the first year of operation, we can see ever more clearly the grandeur of Medvedkin's self-appointed mission: not just to remedy day-to-day problems, but to use cinema to create categories of citizenship. Just as the 'little people' (in Medvedkin's words, the 'invisible heroes') had a role to play in the creation of socialism, so the local community was summoned to fulfil goals for the national good.[30]

The Camel of Shame

The success of Medvedkin's agitational project depended on the manipulation of 'shame', naming incompetent and irresponsible individuals and groups on the screen. In his notes, we find the scribbled observation that 'I must make a film about lack of personal responsibility' – a problem encountered in mines and farms across the territory.[31] 'The force of inertia is a terrible one!' he wrote. 'We came up against it on every journey of the film-train, and we fought tirelessly with it.'[32]

One of the most interesting innovations of the film-train was directly linked to the idea of 'shame'. A screenplay in Medvedkin's archive, dated 1931, shows the development of a figure that can be called the 'camel of shame', an animated figure to be superimposed on material taken from real life. The scenario is comic. In the opening sequence, a camel ('ridiculous and amusing', Medvedkin notes) is tied to the back of a fast-moving train, and trying to keep pace. The camel was, Medvedkin emphasised, strictly not to be 'realistic' – it had to look ridiculous. The train stops at a station, and out of it come film-makers with all their equipment, together with the film's main hero, Murzilk.

As all this unloading is taking place the camel becomes bored, and begins to eat the railway signal system. An irate signalman throws a stone, which pierces the animated camel, so that it begins to deflate like a balloon. Here the film seems to rejoice in its own artifice: Murzilk rushes to help, but is too late – all the air has escaped, and the camel lies pierced and airless on the ground. Murzilk begins, therefore, to blow it back up, and bit by bit we watch the camel rise from the ashes and regain its normal, but ridiculous shape. Murzilk, however, continues to blow, so that the camel eventually begins to float, carrying the hero away with it. In panic, Murzilk punctures it, and they float back down to earth together, landing in an empty street. Walking along the street, they see a sign, which declares that camels are forbidden in this town: the camel bursts into tears (a touch of ironic humour and a sign of Medvedkin's growing familiarity with American comedy can be read in the instruction that 'Out of camel's eyes, like with American film-stars, burst hot tears') and runs away, arriving at a disgracefully disorganised engine repair factory.

It is at this point that the plot's agitational significance becomes clear; the camel moves around the factory, inadvertently rooting out the worst examples of malpractice. This screenplay, then, might be seen as telling the story of the train itself. It arrives in a community and roots out bad practice. The lugubrious camel is happy when it hears of successful sections of the factory, unhappy when they are unsuccessful. At the end of the film it is left in the factory, as a symbol of shame, to be taken away only when the factory has improved its performance.

The idea of the camel was developed during 1931, with a view to use on the film-train that Medvedkin was then trying to organise. In a note attached to the scenario in the archive, Medvedkin writes that the camel is

> conceived as the first in a whole series of drawn, animated comedies of the adventures [*pokhozhdeniiakh* – Medvedkin uses the folkloric term] of a single hero, Murzilk, in connection with the Plan. The principal technical specificity is that the 'camel' and related things will be drawn not on paper, but on transparent sheets of celluloid, which will enable us to *repeat* this comedy as often as we want, changing only the photographic background ('Today the camel is in the Donbass, then in Kharkov, etc.').[33]

Medvedkin's plans for the camel demonstrate two key elements of the train's work. First, they show the importance he ascribed to the concept of 'shame' from his earliest plans for the train. Second, they demonstrate that he envisaged comedy to have an important role to play in the agitational cinema that he proposed. It is clear that the camel did go on to play a role in the train's work – and on the very first of Medvedkin's team's own 'adventures'. A semi-animated film entitled *A Camel Visits the Dnepropetrovsk Steam Locomotive Repair Works*, produced during the first expedition, would seem to have developed out of the earlier screenplay. It would appear that the camel was used only once more in a full 'feature' of this kind, during the expedition to the Donbass steel regions, but it is likely that it did appear in a more minor role in several of the other films.

The value of shame was twofold. Fear of humiliation would encourage improved behaviour. Second, the very notion of 'shame' emphasised the value and necessity of collective activity, denoting a shared community, in which the behaviour of one has direct impact upon the other.[34] Thus, through shame, Medvedkin aimed to make the individual part of a broader community – both local and, ultimately, national. Similarly, the method of setting good example against bad, encouraging the community to identify itself as a competitor in a regional race to fulfil quotas, sought to create reciprocal structures of identity between local communities. Films made in one community – or on one expedition – were added to the film-train's permanent repertoire, for showing to other communities during other trips. On arrival in the Donbass mining region in October 1932, for example, the team launched their campaign with what Medvedkin describes as an initial 'raid' of residential hostels and other meeting places, where they screened films that they had made during the earlier mining expedition. Thus the Donbass miners were drawn into a 'network' of labour and production, summoned to participation in a project that had national significance.

Although little evidence remains of concrete reactions to screenings, and it is not clear how the films were used by communities after the departure of the train, it is certainly the case that copies of each film made in a given community were left in the hands of local administration. Medvedkin recounts how the Mine Committee of the Krivbass region purchased three films 'for future work'.[35] After the Donbass trip, at least seventy films were left in the hands of factories and other administrative bodies. Although Medvedkin was later to bemoan what he perceived as insufficiently serious use of the films as educational propaganda after the departure of the train, it seems clear that the films did enter the entertainment repertoire of small local communities.

It was not enough to encourage discussion and to aid the taking of positive decisions, however; what was needed, of course, was to ensure that promises were kept. Medvedkin instigated surprise 'raids' on communities previously visited, to ensure that they were fulfilling the targets that they had set themselves. The threat of the camera eye was an ever-present reminder of the risk of public shame – if you weren't fulfilling your resolutions, it would find you.

Impact

In an article written in 1933, reflecting on the previous year's work on the train, Medvedkin complained vociferously about the lack of press attention that the train had received.[36] While it is true that there seems to have been no mention of the train in any national newspaper, there was some coverage in film journals during the first year. During the first expedition to Dnepropetrovsk, *Kino* published regular short pieces about the train's progress, usually in the form of telegrams sent by team members themselves. We read, for example, of the extraordinarily rapid production of one film as 'the first experience of the "assault brigade" of film work'.[37] This phrase, echoing Medvedkin's insistence on military vocabulary in his own descriptions of the train's work, confirms the train's place within the consolidating hierarchy of Stalinist production. Prioritising productivity over creativity, it inscribes it into the hegemonic discourses of the Five-Year Plan. By September, a regular 'Letter from the Film-train' was published every few weeks. On 18 September a short essay praised the train for having developed 'a popular, easily intelligible, expressive film language, using the production epic, journalistic genres, caricature, the devices of posters'.[38]

Medvedkin was not content, however; for him, the train was a phenomenon of national significance, and should be recognised as such in the central press. In January 1933, returning from the Donbass, he left the train, and a few months later published an essay in which he stated clearly his belief that it had deserved greater institutional support and bemoaned the failure of the cinematic administration to realise that film could be a 'weapon in mass labour'.[39] Few of the films were put on national release – perhaps because of the dismal reality of the state of Soviet industry and agriculture that Medvedkin was so concerned to improve. His images of real people, in real places, in real time, were – whether he liked it or not – too dangerous for the regime, and risked destabilising the propaganda project of which he was supposedly a part. This was the fundamental ambivalence that characterised Medvedkin's project, succinctly and movingly expressed by Chris Marker: 'Armed with your socialist good conscience, but never cheating with the image.' Inadvertently or not, but these honest images nevertheless revealed the flaws of the very world Medvedkin promoted.

After Medvedkin's departure the train languished in Moscow for five months, before finding a new 'commander' in the form of Iakov Bliokh, who had worked with Eisenstein on *The Battleship Potemkin* [Bronenosets Potemkin, 1925]. It carried out a further six expeditions over the subsequent three years – the same number as it had managed in a single year under Medvedkin's Stakhanovite regime. By 1935 the cinematic bureaucracy had changed its tune, and Boris Shumiatsky (head of the Central Cinematrographic Administration [GUK]) became official sponsor of the train. Its project, however, underwent significant change. In a statement of its 'Tasks for 1935', the organisers of the train proclaimed their intention henceforward to reflect local details *as they would be interesting for the public*. This indicates a marked shift towards a more touristic gaze.

> The spectator is interested in knowing how people in the Fergana Valley live, what the Khorezm Oasis looks like, what Nagornyi Karabakh is [...], how people hunt for tigers, how people live on the Murmansk coast. As we move around 'on wheels' we spend time in all these places, see all of this, and we have a duty to show it all to the spectator, who has long hoped for that genre which we call the 'local interest' film.[40]

The interventionist, agitational remit of Medvedkin's train was replaced, then, with precisely the kind of entertainment and passive 'interest' that he had always sought to avoid. The real experiment of the film-train was at an end, and (as we will see in Chapter 7) Medvedkin had to wait some forty years for its extraordinary innovation to be recognised.

3. *Happiness*

After his work on the train, Medvedkin's credentials as a director had evidently improved. He was able to get money for a full-length feature film for the new Moscow film studio, Mosfilm. Released in 1935, *Happiness* was a continuation of Medvedkin's search for a new form for Soviet comedy. 'Cinema scarcely touches the riches of Russian folklore,' he explained; with *Happiness*, he would appropriate the stylistic techniques of old Russian popular culture to create a film that was highly relevant to the present.[1] It was this attempt to blend the old and the new that gave birth to the startlingly original hybrid that is Medvedkin's masterpiece.

Happiness is structured around a proverbial riddle, which provides the title for its first 'chapter': 'What is Happiness?' Its four 'chapters' follow the adventures of the peasant Khmyr and his wife Anna over an overtly unrealistic time-frame that carries them from an unspecified pre-Revolutionary period into the collectivised countryside of Stalin's Russia. At the beginning of the film Khmyr and Anna are poor peasants, struggling to create a homestead, envying their rich neighbour his life of plenty. After the death of his father Khmyr sets off to 'find happiness', and stumbles upon a full purse that has been dropped by a drunken merchant. His luck ends there, however; even with a horse, a hut and a plentiful harvest, Khmyr and Anna are at the mercy of society. We see their evil neighbour Foka, together with soldiers, priests, prisoners and bureaucrats (symbolically representative of the taxes paid by the peasant to the state) taking away their money and their grain.

Eventually, Khmyr is so full of despair that he decides to die, dismantling his own outbuildings to find the wood for his coffin. Here too he is thwarted, however. Soldiers arrive to assert his duty, as subject of the Russian Empire, to stay alive, for, as an intertitle proclaims, 'If the peasant dies, who will feed

Russia?' They seize him and carry him away to prison. At this point the film moves forward in time, to the present of the early 1930s, and to the collectivised countryside of Stalin's Russia. After years of hardship, Khmyr has 'lost confidence in happiness', and has become idle and selfish, a comic 'fool' with no place in the Soviet world. At the end of the film, however, he is redeemed: when the evil Foka (also transported unaged into the future) tries to destroy the collective's horses, Khmyr is galvanised into action and becomes a hero. His future in the new world is assured.

*   *   *

With *Happiness*, Medvedkin responded to a need – much discussed in the cinema press of the time – for films about collectivisation.[2] After the film-train experience, he was only too aware of the difficult reality of rural life in Soviet Russia. The question was how to use film to improve it.[3] In an essay published alongside the screenplay, Medvedkin offered his solution, and provided a substantial ideological justification for his new film. It would focus, he said, on a common social type that he called the 'left-behind collective farm worker' (*otstalyi kolkhoznik*). These were peasants caught between two social orders (pre- and post-Revolutionary), and unwilling to engage with the concept of the collective's shared goods. This was the legacy of serfdom: the perpetual hardship and suffering of the peasantry had given birth to a powerful 'dream of a well-fed life'; poverty had bred a paradoxical obsession with property. And this obsession threatened the success of the collectivisation project.[4]

The original title for *Happiness*, *The Possessors* [Stiazhateli], expressed this directly: Khmyr and Anna aspire to be 'possessors', to cultivate their own land, and the purpose of the film is to reveal that aspiration as misplaced.[5] Thus it is structured around questions of property and ownership. Its narrative momentum is initially provided by jealousy: Khmyr, his grandfather and his wife peer through a hole in an fence as food flies, as if by magic, into the mouth of their well-fed neighbour Foka (Figure 1). The desire to taste such food leads to tragedy (to the grandfather's untimely death as he tries to scale Foka's fences, brave his guard dog and break through his padlocks), and it is this lit-eral nail in the coffin of indigence that prompts Khmyr's journey – an explicit search for a better life.

Stumbling upon the bulging purse, Khmyr sets about 'possessing', and Medvedkin presents an affecting and ironic picture of the peasant's humble ambition. He buys himself a dappled horse (with a comically rapacious appetite), and encloses his forlorn wooden hut with enormous fences and padlocks that proudly imitate the forbidding grandeur of those of Foka; he even acquires a tiny and ineffectual hound (a parodic echo of the neighbour's fierce guard dog). From the beginning, however, things are comically askew: Khmyr and Anna's hut is a symbol of misplaced aspiration, of dream rather than reality. A stork settles on the roof in parodic recognition of the process of homemaking, their dappled horse is so determined to eat that he makes for the hut's thatched roof,[6] and, eventually, their wealth is stolen away. Thieves breaking through those vicious fences and enormous padlocks are indignant to find only empty coffers, for, as Medvedkin explained, 'in the peasant home trunks, bolts, locks, guard dogs and fences more often than not protected wretched rags and indigence'.[7]

After Khmyr is transported to the present, his dream of 'a well-fed life' (what Medvedkin called the peasant's 'petty-proprietorial psychology')[8] is a threat to the success of the collective project. His sense of displacement ('I'm not allowed to live in the old way, and can't live in the new') can be exploited by Foka (now a kulak) and his evil cronies. This, for Medvedkin, was the principal problem: the Russian peasant was not evil, he said, but his 'desperate and often concealed disorientation leads to absurd relapses into the desire to accumulate and safeguard personal property [*stiazhatel'stvo*]', and this

1. Foka (*Happiness*, 1935)

weakness could 'be masterfully exploited by the kulak as the chaff to destroy collective labour'.[9]

Medvedkin's vocabulary here was steeped in the socio-political rhetoric of the day. Khymr is one of the 'former people' (*byvshie liudi*) described by Stalin in a speech to the Party in January 1933, whose determination to remain trapped in the attitudes of the past hindered the transformation of society. For Medvedkin, this social relevance made the film 'Socialist Realist', in line with the official cultural doctrine that had been adopted at the famous First Congress of Soviet Writers in 1934.[10] Literature and cinema alike should tell simple stories about socialist heroes, narrating the 'real' romanticism that was Soviet reality.

For all its creator's attempts to inscribe it into the emergent discourses of Socialist Realism, however, the remarkable *Happiness* cannot easily be categorised within the consolidating trends of Soviet cinema of the period. Although it has an overarching linear structure that tracks Khmyr's gradual transformation into a heroic member of the collective, this plot does not dominate the film. Instead, the film is an episodic series of adventures, both comic and tragic.[11] And its remarkable folkloric aesthetics, its hyperbole and stylisation, carry it far from Socialist Realism's sanctioned 'revolutionary romanticism'.

Folklore

The folkloric roots of Medvedkin's tale are evident from its opening sequences. With titles dividing his four 'chapters', Medvedkin inscribes the film self-consciously into popular narrative tradition. It is, as the first intertitle proclaims, a 'tale of the hapless possessor Khmyr, of his wife-horse, Anna, of the well-fed neighbour Foka, and also of the priest, the nun and other scarecrows, dedicated to the last idler in the collective farm'. This folkloric style is maintained in the film's other intertitles, many of which are proverbial, and even rhymed. Often ironic and always self-conscious, the intertitles function almost as captions, sometimes enabling satirical asides ('but the horse was a glutton, and Khmyr had no fodder'), sometimes adding to the self-conscious stylisation of the film's folkloric mode.

Throughout the film, Medvedkin's debt to the narratives and characters of folklore is overt. Khmyr (played by the same Petr Zinoviev who had been the eponymous Duren of Medvedkin's 1931 short) emerges clearly out of the folkloric prototype of Ivan the Fool, the lazy but good-hearted hero of many a tale, and a figure familiar in Medvedkin's early comedies. Like Ivan, Khmyr sets off on a journey: to find his 'happiness'. This positions the film squarely within a folkloric genre. Vladimir Propp suggests that folkloric narratives are generally structured around two spatial models: the home and the journey. The hero's departure from the domestic space initiates a journey, a series of trials and adventures, which concludes in a return to and reappropriation of the home.[12] This journey provides the temporal and spatial coordinates of the narrative.

Happiness appears at first glance to conform to this model, but with ironic twists. Khmyr, on his journey, approaches a crossroads marked by a dead tree that seems to be pointing in various directions. On the tree is carved a message: 'If you go left, you will die of death, if you go straight on – you'll expire. If you go right, you won't die, but you won't live either.' All three options represent death; this riddle has no solution. In a parodic take on the folk tale and its magical riddles, Medvedkin's message is clear: for the pre-Revolutionary peasant, there was no happy ending.

This fate notwithstanding, Khmyr's initial quest comes to a disconcertingly rapid and successful conclusion. Thereafter, his folkloric 'journey' is metaphorical, a path through history that transforms the humble and virtuous Ivan of folklore into the peasant-everyman. His adventures take place in a world populated by, in Medvedkin's words, 'odious Russian figures' – familiar characters from early satire and folklore such as the fairy-tale witch Baba Iaga, the greedy priest, the horse thief and the extortioner. The moral binaries of folklore – of richness and poverty, good and evil – structure the narrative.[13] Foka the neighbour, in particular, is a fairy-tale villain; we first see him placed centrally within the shot framed by a tree, seated at his groaning table with its white tablecloth, as food flies miraculously into his mouth (the very incarnation of the idea of plenty). Throughout the film the white of his beard and hair attracts the light of the film, and has the effect of making him appear almost supernatural.

In the contemporary sections of the film the timeless world of folklore collides with a recognisable socio-political context. Foka, a folkloric 'extortioner' in the pre-Revolutionary sections of the film, is transposed into a kulak. He is ever more devilish, materialising out of thin air to work his evil magic. He and the other misfits (a visually stylised group that Medvedkin described as the 'swindlers') become 'saboteurs', key enemies of the Soviet project. In the irreverent tradition of Russian secular folklore, religion is a soft target for Medvedkin's satire in both periods: priests are shown to be money-grabbing and immoral (demanding extra cash to bury Khmyr's grandfather, fighting to get hold of the merchant's dropped purse, stealing grain from the collective, etc.), and in one of the most memorable scenes in the film the nuns that appear to steal Khmyr's harvest wear transparent black habits through which their naked breasts cheekily belie their sanctity (Figure 2). In the collective farm, these religious figures are no different from the other villains who conspire to destroy progress.

The Poetics of Folklore

Such details notwithstanding, the principal innovation of Medvedkin's use of folklore is stylistic rather than thematic. It extends beyond detail, into 'the internal processing of the material'.[14] Valeri Fomin, who has explored the relationship between film and folklore in some detail, marks *Happiness* as the first attempt at creating a quite new cinematic genre: one that used the poetics of folklore.[15] The project was an ambitious one. The intrinsically mimetic quality of cinema as a photographic medium seemed – and may still seem – inimical to folkloric stylisation.

This problem is most evident in questions of setting. The folk tale provides no detail except that which is essential to the story: in Propp's words, 'There is no attempt to describe landscape. Forest, river, sea, steppes and city walls are mentioned when the hero jumps over or crosses them, but the narrator is indifferent to the beauty of the landscape.'[16] Medvedkin's solution to this problem was a pointed rejection of cinema's photographic qualities. In the first version of the screenplay for *Happiness*, he described the proposed opening frame thus: 'Rus. A meadow. A chapel. A dead tree. The skeleton of a horse. Boulders.'[17] This shot, which was to be five metres in length (lasting

2. Corrupt religion (*Happiness*, 1935)

some fifteen seconds), would set up a framework for the ensuing narrative, providing only the most vital details of the filmic space. Slow and sparse in detail, it is indicative of the broader poetics of the film. As Khmyr sets off on his journey, for example, we see only that which we need for the narrative: a path, a tree, a river and a bridge (on which the priest and nun will fight). There is no background, no landscape; 'real' space becomes unreal.

Viktor Demin describes this stylistic peculiarity as Medvedkin's 'naked' frame, claiming that 'only this extreme laconicism can make the visible world into a folk tale'.[18] This notion of a 'laconic' style is essential to understanding Medvedkin's technique, for it enables his careful balance between the real and the unreal. Emptying the frame of detail, he achieves a cinematic equivalent of folklore's geographical placelessness. Landscape is avoided: there are few panoramic establishing shots, and the narrative mode is articulated via a predominance of middle-range shots, avoiding any real sense of place. The film's location is marked only by the continuing presence of a lone, leafless and rather twisted tree, and by Khmyr's tumbledown hut; together, these images provide a sense of continuity through the film.

Placeless, the space of *Happiness* becomes one of action and experience. As we see Khmyr and his dappled horse pulling a plough up a hill (and when, after the horse refuses to continue, the impressive Anna straps herself into its place), for example, Medvedkin uses the visual potential of film to offer a vivid representation of the experience. The hill is overtly unrealistic – simply a large boulder in an otherwise empty frame. It exists only in the context of the protagonists' ascent. And, as they climb, it is reduced to a two-dimensional diagonal line that bisects the frame (Figure 3). In this way, with 'realistic' landscape rejected, the spectator is drawn into a more graphic awareness of the physical experience itself. Elsewhere, the space of the film materialises according to the needs of the narrative. When Anna collapses from fatigue after her ploughing exertions, for example, Khmyr bedecks her with flowers. Where does he find them? In an opulent flower garden, which appears suddenly out of nowhere amidst the otherwise barren landscape.

Time

The unreality of the film's landscape means that we are unaware even of seasonal change: Khmyr's bumper harvest arrives apparently out of the blue into a world in which nature appears largely uniform and – if the recurring dead tree is anything to go by – even infertile (despite the flowers). This absence of time is typical of Medvedkin's folkloric antecedents. In the folk tale, Propp suggests, the journey (which is cyclical) provides the only temporal and spatial axis for the tale.[19] The time of the tale is outside history; it is premised solely on experience: 'There is no general concept of time in folklore. Just as there is only empirical space, there is only empirical time, measured not by dates, days or years, but by the personages' actions. [...] Time as a form of thought does not seem to exist.'[20] In similar terms, Dmitri Likhachev has described the time of the Russian folk tale as 'enclosed time', which does not exist outside the limits of the tale.[21]

The rejection of linear time in *Happiness* enables a cavalier approach to Russian history, and Medvedkin juxtapose two epochs, pre- and post-Revolutionary, without clear demarcation. His characters are transported, miraculously unaged, across time. Signalling the transition from the pre- to post-Revolutionary sections of the film, an intertitle informs us of the passing of time; it does so, however, in a way that explicitly confuses rather than stabilising. 'For thirty-three years Khmyr was beaten, on twelve fronts he was shot at, and seven times killed...And so he lost confidence in Happiness.'

This lack of temporal verisimilitude parodies the passing of time in folklore, and contributes to the film's stylised mode, but it is also a highly contemporary, politically astute appropriation of the folkloric 'Once upon a

3. Climbing the hill (*Happiness*, 1935)

time...' The folkloric poetics of the film enable Medvedkin to comment on the collision between two different temporal categories: official, historical time (which is more or less linear and measurable; government time) and lived time (time as it is experienced; peasant time). This is part of his attack on the pre-Revolutionary regime. Those thirty-three years take us, implicitly, from 1902 or thereabouts to 1935, and we emerge into the world of Stalinist collectivisation. The five military fronts described must surely include the Russo–Japanese War, the First World War and the Russian Civil War, inscribing Khmyr into a history that is at once unreal – and horrifyingly real. He becomes everyman – the peasant at the mercy of history; and the irrelevance of historical time in the poetics of the film is balanced by its lurking presence, intruding upon characters' lives.

This point is made with sinister clarity when Khmyr 'decides to die'. As he builds his coffin from the wood of his tumbledown hut, he is visited by a motley assemblage of caricatured figures, a grotesque microcosm of Russian society, determined to stop his 'unauthorised' death. 'Who gave you the right to die?' an intertitle demands. Thematically, then, private and public time collide. As a chattel, the property of others, the peasant does not own his own body, and cannot control his own time.

The Grotesque

At this point the rebellious Khmyr is carried off by a troop of soldiers in grotesquely oversized masks (Figure 4), their mouths frozen in a circle of permanent outrage – a disturbing premonition of Walt Disney's Mickey Mouse blended with the threatening features of the 'Mongol horde' of Andrei Bely's apocalyptic novel, *Petersburg* (1916). This is one of the most chilling episodes in the film, as the soldiers' uniform and deranged 'o' seem to encapsulate the violent authority of state power. 'Medvedkin here scales the heights of genuine grotesque,' wrote Eisenstein in his review of the film; 'beneath the savagery and absurdity of a cardboard jowl reproduced on every solider you could discern the terrible, moribund face of the regime. Pure Shchedrin.'[22]

This comparison is apt: the nineteenth-century satiric writer Saltykov-Shchedrin was well known for his evocations of banal and mindless authority. One of the most disturbing episodes in his parodic chronicle *A History of a Town* [Istoriia odnogo goroda, 1869–1879] tells of a town governor whose head is a machine, stuck in the endless repetition of the brutal and intolerant 'I won't stand for it'. Like that mechanised head, the masked soldiers in *Happiness* appear as puppets, mechanised and unresponsive, and as such they are at once comic and horrifying. As Henri Bergson observes, the comic potential of the puppet stems from man's innate and deep-seated fear of the automaton, of the human body deprived of will, reduced to the mechanical.[23] Medvedkin was evidently well aware of the impact of the mask as a device; at a meeting in 1930 he stated his intention to exploit its potentially disturbing power in cinematic close-up. Seen here at middle-range and close up, the mask manages to express a double meaning: it is a metaphor of brutality read by the spectator, and at the same time a visualisation of Khmyr's own, terrified vision of the force that controls his life.

Stylisation

Medvedkin's use of exaggeration and caricature was rooted in the folk tradition of the *lubok*, which he named as the principal influence on his cinematic vision. The *lubok*, first appearing in Russia in the seventeenth century, was a woodcut – a cartoon-like illustration with short explanatory (usually comic and often satiric) text below.[24] *Luboks* were predominantly two-dimensional tableaux in which a static image captured a moment of action, simplified and exaggerated to convey a message.

4. Khmyr and the soldiers (*Happiness*, 1935)

Consideration of the visual codes of the *lubok* is helpful in understanding the poetics of *Happiness*. This was a silent film by choice made at a time when sound cinema was very much a possibility. Consciously avoiding the putative 'realism' of sound and dialogue, Medvedkin used his titles, like the captions in a *lubok*, to comment on and frame visual images.[25] Visually, he sought to make the cinematic frame appear, like the *lubok*, as 'a painting on a panel...a panel in a newspaper'.[26] His montage is relatively slow, such that individual frames may last for up to twenty or thirty seconds (five to ten metres of film). Thus they too serve almost as tableaux, and the film's emphasis is on composition and framing.

Similarly, the 'primitive' visual codes of the *lubok* (which had been the source of inspiration for the 'neoprimitive' visual artists Mikhail Larionov and Natalia Goncharova during the 1910s, as well as for the ROSTA window campaigns) are echoed in Medvedkin's 'naked' landscapes. His long, sometimes motionless, and highly stylised shots are organised geometrically, making striking use of the contrasts of light and dark. In the opening sequence, for example, the frame is bisected by the dramatic diagonal of Foka's wall, which divides it visually into a striking opposition of black and white, lit from above and from the right.

The human body, too, is enlisted in the film's visual language: these long tableau shots frequently rely for their impact on the human body. Without dialogue, characters convey meaning through gesture, often captured in silhouette, and the plasticity of the body plays an important part in the impact of the frame. In the opening scene, for example, much of the geometry is created by the opposition of Khmyr's bent body, peering through the hole in the fence, with Anna's characteristically statuesque upright form.

All this has both visual and metaphorical impact. Throughout the film, physical appearance is meaning-bearing. Anna is highly stylised as a statuesque, almost iconic vision of 'woman' (a kind of Mother Russia, perhaps?),[27] frequently pictured standing still, inspiring both awe and fear in her husband – and the spectator – with the powerful kiss (lifting the diminutive Zinoviev off his feet) with which she sends him off on his quest for 'happiness'. Elsewhere, visual contrast (and satiric impact) are provided by a remarkably short, rotund, long-bearded priest and a tall, thin witch-like nun, dressed all in black with a pointed chin and protruding warts, and by the caricatured forms of the 'villains' who seek to sabotage the collective farm. The real bodies of Medvedkin's actors acquire a cartoon-like quality, and, in keeping with this caricatured aesthetic, human movements are marked by a particular blend of fluidity and stillness. As priest and nun fight like tigers to get hold of the merchant's lost purse (later to become Khmyr's fistfull of 'happiness'), for example, sequences of rapid movement are interrupted by periodic pauses –

still frames in which the actors' bodies are caught in shaped poses (reminiscent of Meyerhold's system of 'biomechanics'; Figure 5). Throughout the film the pace is dictated by a remarkable synthesis of stillness and energy.

Metaphor made Flesh

The explicit stylisation of the human body is part of the fairy-tale logic of the film's poetics, in which important objects, or people, are bigger than unimportant ones. As the grandfather struggles with Foka's padlock in the opening sequence, the padlock is as large as, or larger than, his head; when two priests arrive to persuade Khmyr out of his project of death, the more important of them is almost twice the size of the insignificant local priest. This is the most extraordinary quality of *Happiness*: the visual surface of the film can be read as a sequence of metaphors made flesh. Indeed, the very premise of the film is at once abstract and concrete: Khmyr, after all, finds 'happiness', in the form of a bulging purse, and carries it home to his Anna. In another example, as his father dies from shock in the opening sequence of the film, we see a puff of smoke emerge from his mouth and rise up into the air: literally, his 'last breath' (Figure 6).

5. The fight (*Happiness*, 1935)

Medvedkin's remarkable ability to visualise the abstract, and to make the film 'speak', is similarly evident in peculiarities of technique: at key moments in the film (during the funeral of Khmyr's father, for example, and after the first 'theft' of his harvest) the camera adopts a disconcerting aerial perspective, reminiscent of the techniques of German expressionism (the influence of 'Caligarism' on Soviet cinema was considered dangerous in the cinema press of the period). This de-familiarises the scene, in a visual equivalent of the moral injustice of the situation. Avoiding realism, the poetics of the film act as an ongoing commentary, providing the principal level of meaning on which the film operates.[28]

This is particularly clear in the scene after Anna's exhausted collapse, when a distraught Khmyr bedecks her with flowers and sits with his accordion to sing to her. As he sings, Medvedkin inserts a daydream sequence, in which we see *into* our protagonist's imagination. He and his beloved are miraculously transformed into a fairy-tale king and queen, seated at a richly decorated table, which groans beneath plentiful food and wine (Figure 7). 'If I were Tsar,' Khmyr sings, 'I would eat dripping on dripping.'[29]

The scene is self-consciously artificial: Khmyr and Anna's costumes make no pretence of being other than fancy dress, and the set is strikingly

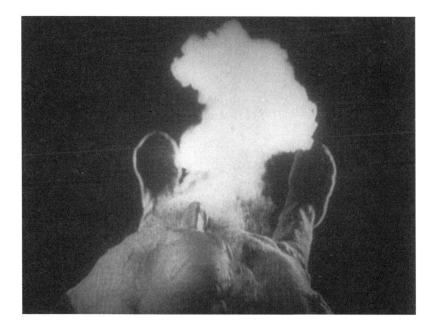

6. The last breath (*Happiness*, 1935)

two-dimensional – reminiscent, as Izvolov has observed, of the 'inverse perspective of a Russian icon'.[30] Just as the Russian icon traditionally offers a kind of flattened perspective, so in this film, in the words of Demin, 'the spectator is presented with unexpected proportions in relation to perspective; there is no point in the centre which unites them', creating a kind of 'fairy-tale space'.[31] Against this fairy-tale space, the protagonists are shot in stylised close-up as they eat.

Naïvety

Here, as elsewhere in the film, poetics carry meaning. The visual structure of the sequence is, implicitly, that of Khmyr's dream, and of his imagination. His vision of the 'life of a tsar' is explicitly naïve, circumscribed by the fairy-tale frames of reference that are available to him. He is incapable of conceptualising it in other, more 'realistic' terms. The spectator, drawn into this fantasy world, is given a double vision: we look *through* Khmyr's eyes, as well as at him. This is the fundamental originality of the film: with its stylised folk poetics, *Happiness* is at once *about* the peasant view of the world and a realisation *of* it.

7. Khmyr's dream (*Happiness*, 1935)

In the first draft of the screenplay for the film Medvedkin anticipated that the dream sequence would be in colour, and, indeed, a colour version of this sequence was produced in Mosfilm (the first colour production of the studio).[32] It would seem that the experiment was unsuccessful, however, and it has not been preserved.[33] In an extraordinary feat of self-justification, Medvedkin later even claimed that the poor quality of the colour episode was adequate to express the 'limited' nature of Khmyr's dream: 'At that time the peasant could not dream of anything multicoloured and beautiful. His dream was limited, and in that the technology helped.'[34]

The explicit sympathy with which Medvedkin treats the 'limitations' of Khmyr's imagination raises questions about his treatment of his protagonist throughout the film. Like any good satirist, Medvedkin sought to manipulate the spectator's relationship with his hero: 'I am not afraid of being harsh; in every episode I will relate to Khmyr warmly and intimately, as if to my closest friend, and will create a sympathetic relation to him in the spectator.' Khmyr is to be at once loved and despised, recognised and mocked, and it is in this shifting relationship that the satirical force of the film lies. As Medvedkin wrote in 1933, 'I laugh at him, but I know that in the near future he will become one of us, so I do not castigate him, only laugh'.[35]

In fact, this blend of sympathy and satire is fundamental to the film's structure, part of its very poetics. Although the ideological narrative suggests that Khmyr's foolishness must be overcome, the effect of the film's comedy, and of its stylised poetics, is to immerse the spectator within the very naïve world-view that it ostensibly seeks to criticise. The simplicity of Khmyr's dream is affecting; he is Ivan the Fool, and the film's moral hierarchy links stupidity with virtue. In the end, he is a hero not despite, but because of, his naïvety. And, in visual terms, his world-view is that of the film.

'Truth' in Hyperbole

Medvedkin was explicit about his use of ancient precedent in *Happiness*, but claimed that those who had read the screenplay as a 'mere' *lubok* or fairy tale were wrong. 'Taking material from folklore,' he explained, 'the film reworks it by means of hyperbole into a realistic conception.'[36] Defending the screenplay of *The Possessors* before filming began, he made a similar claim: 'I wanted to construct something realistic. But I approached realism not via naturalism, but via the grotesque and hyperbole.'[37] These apparently paradoxical statements are the key to Medvedkin's ambition: to achieve greater social relevance, a greater 'reality', through the use of exaggeration and stylisation.

On screen, Medvedkin suggested, apparently 'improbable circumstances' would acquire a kind of hyper-reality, and hence social impact. Describing

Khmyr and Anna's hut in an early screenplay, for example, Medvedkin writes: 'the little hut is improbable. Not a house, but an evil parody of human habitation from the Middle Ages.'[38] Some details must be socially 'true' (it must be 'made from logs and rotten wood', for example), but the principal function of the hut is as symbol, evoking the film's ideological meaning. It is this combination of the real and unreal that one critic has called Medvedkin's 'parodic-fairytale' aesthetic.[39] Faced with a scene that hovers between the real and the unreal, the spectator is thrown into a kind of double-consciousness, and thus, Medvedkin claimed, becomes receptive to the higher meaning of the film. Real 'truth', he suggested, lay not in a picture of reality *as it was*, but in the ideological 'truth' of the film's message. *Happiness* was 'real' or 'truthful' not in detail but in overall subject (*siuzhetnost'*), and in social relevance.

Signs of the Times

Medvedkin was clearly aware, however, that he was stretching the definition of Socialist Realism to its limit. Seeking to avoid the criticisms that had been levelled at his earlier satiric films (see Chapter 1), he tried to ensure that he included realistic, positive examples to balance the satiric hyperbole of the film. In the contemporary sections of the film, hyperbole is toned down. Here, aesthetics encode ideological appropriateness: Foka and the other misfit enemies of collectivisation remain stylised – implicitly trapped in the past. Anna, however, is less stylised, pictured more 'realistically' as a contented member of the collective farm and a record-breaking worker (Figure 8), and her heroism is contrasted with her husband's disaffection.

Khmyr, meanwhile, is 'the worst collective-farm water carrier', and we see him and his recalcitrant dappled horse asleep 'on the job' (with comically mirrored crossed legs). In the context of the collective, Khmyr's failings are more pronounced – and more comic – than in the film's earlier sections. In one incident, he and his ineffectual hound are left to guard the farm's grain supply, and defend it from the swindler-saboteurs. He is easily distracted, however, and is tricked into trying to stop a sheep eating his lettuces, while thieves literally pick up the grain hut and carry it off. The little guard dog, chained to the hut, is carried away after them, barking desperately as its little legs struggle to keep up. It is Anna, of course, who saves the day, using water-melons to attack the saboteurs in the film's most straightforward episode of slapstick comedy. Decisively vanquished, the villains retreat; one of them (the same nun/witch who appeared in the pre-Revolutionary landscape) attempts to hang herself on a moving windmill, in a dramatic shot that shows her crow-like body hanging silhouetted against an empty frame (Figure 9). Medvedkin's

8. Anna in the new world (*Happiness*, 1935)

9. Nun in despair (*Happiness*, 1935)

down-to-earth humour, however, dictates that tragedy is avoided when her suicide attempt fails, and she skulks off, lighting a cigarette.

The remarkable sight of the moving hut with legs in this scene recalls the folkloric witch Baba Iaga, whose famous hut on chicken's legs was able to uproot itself and walk wherever she wished to be. In a characteristic blend of the modern and archaic, it also evokes some of the more Utopian of early Soviet building proposals: the poet Khlebnikov, for example, proposed mobile housing pods that would enable easy travel, and a group of architects named the Disurbanists planned to eliminate the city by providing self-assembly homes transported from place to place by car.[40] This mix of cultural references is characteristic of Medvedkin, and particularly pronounced in the modern-day sections of the film, when the timeless pace of folklore collides with the rhythm of modernity.

Khmyr's battle in the final sections of the film is a fundamental one: between his personal, private need for 'possession' and the needs of the collective. This conflict is dramatised when Foka attempts to convert the disaffected Khmyr to his evil cause, and to involve him in his plot to set fire to the collective's stables. It is this that provides the spur for our hero's awakening; shocked by the horror of the deed, he attempts to save the horses from the leaping flames. To distract him from altruism, Foka lights a second fire – this time in Khmyr's homestead. Thus our hero is forced to choose between personal and collective good. The moment at which he chooses the latter, letting his own house burn as he rescues the shared horses, marks his transformation into a member of the collective – and, implicitly, his passage into the present.

For Eisenstein, this scene demonstrated Medvedkin's unique discovery of a Soviet form of comedy. 'Today I have seen how the Bolshevik laughs,' Eisenstein wrote, explicitly passing the mantle of Soviet comedy onto Medvedkin. 'Medvedkin has resolved the problem of our humour in the same way that I would have done, had I been filming it and making it!'[41] Using the example of Khmyr's dash between the two fires, Eisenstein suggested that Medvedkin had managed to adapt Chaplinesque visual humour to the social and political demands of Soviet comedy, dramatising the conflict between personal and collective property.[42] 'A Chaplin gag is individually illogical,' he wrote, whereas: 'a Medvedkin gag is *socially* illogical' (my emphasis).[43] This crucial difference was Medvedkin's triumph.

Eisenstein's comments echo those of Vladimir Sutyrin, made in discussion of Medvedkin's short comedies some four years earlier, in 1931.[44] Sutyrin had made explicit comparison between Chaplin as 'fool' and Russia's Ivan the Fool. Chaplin's 'foolishness', he claimed, was marked by passivity and a deep-rooted loneliness; by contrast, Ivan was active, with many helpers and well-wishers aiding his journey through life. These differences echo, of course, fundamental distinctions between the individualist America and collective Russia: as such, Charlie is a tragic figure, and Ivan is not. For tragedy has no place in Soviet Russia. As such, *Happiness* concludes with Khmyr affiliated to the collective, and he and Anna have a celebratory trip to the city, where he sheds his old peasant garb for a smart new suit and a different kind of 'happiness'.

Or so it would seem...

Culminating in a visit to the city, *Happiness* would seem to conform to more mainstream cinema of the 1930s, in which the hero's success in the local space was frequently rewarded by recognition from the metropolis. In this case, however, Medvedkin's vision is typically askew, and the visit to the city is one of comic adventure rather than triumph. Our fool is still a fool – he gets caught in revolving doors, falls over and drops things. Khmyr's ostensible move into modernity is graphically incomplete: in the department store, transformed by a new outfit with his beard shaved off, he cannot find a way to get rid of his old clothes – symbols of his peasanthood. Every time he tries to throw them away, he is foiled; shop assistants and policemen conspire to ensure that they stay with him. It is only when Khmyr and Anna return to the village that a solution is found, and they leave their forlorn bundle to be stolen by the increasingly desperate villains. This is a final reversal of power, signalling Khmyr's victory over the forces that oppressed him, and the film ends with hilarity as he and Anna have, literally, the last laugh.

Thus, the visit to the city seems gently to parody rather than to conform. As such, it is part of a set of subtle parodic hints that pepper the modern sections of the film. Medvedkin's screenplay stated his intention to provide a vision of the glories of the Soviet future. Seeming to anticipate the idealisation of modern agriculture in the 'collective farm musicals' of Ivan Pyrev and others who were to appear later in the decade, he described a 'column of shining, magnificent machines' to signal the transition to Soviet reality.[45] In practice, however, this celebration of modernity is curiously discordant.

Medvedkin was a man whose business was images, a former propaganda worker more than aware of the symbolic armature of Soviet culture, and in this film he seems to make explicit reference to other films about the countryside. Dovzhenko's *Earth* [1930], for example, had dramatised a tragic battle between peasant 'possessors' and representatives of the 'new', Soviet world, and Eisenstein and Grigori Alexandrov's *The General Line* [1929] similarly dealt with the difficult transition of the village from 'backwardness' to modernity. Medvedkin's leafless, barren landscape might be read as a rebuttal of the romanticism of Dovzhenko's lyrical *Earth*, in which the Russian peasantry, old and new alike, is pictured in a poetic and even organic relation with nature. Khmyr and Anna are given no such solace.

In both *Earth* and *The General Line*, moreover, technology (the tractor, the milk-separator, etc.) was celebrated as an agent of liberation, a symbol of the enlightenment of the modern age. Medvedkin's representation of the mechanisation of the contemporary era, however, is out of kilter. The archetypal tractor driver, new hero of the collectivised countryside, appears in *Happiness* in a different, unheroic guise. In one scene, for example, he is easily lured from his duty by the evil Foka. Tempted by vodka (in a modern version of the folkloric magic tablecloth, miraculously replenishing itself), the tractor driver abandons his machine, and his tractor – ostensible saviour of the peasant – carries on alone and becomes a terrible marauding parody of the machine that is supposed to be man's friend. In what seems like an explicit inversion of a scene in *The General Line*, where tractors are shown in synchronised harmony creating perfect circles in a field, this tractor encircles its drunken master and then heads off across the fields, escaping the control of the collective-farm workers and almost falling off a cliff (which appears, suddenly and conveniently, in Medvedkin's space of action). Its circles, perhaps, are a symbol of backwardness, of technology regressed, and its headlong and uncontrolled dash across the fields is a comic rebuttal of the linear symbolism of the perfectly ploughed field.

These parodic hints, subtle as they are, add further texture to the dense network of cultural reference that is *Happiness*. They are part of the intense self-consciousness that is the film's most fundamental quality. As such, Medvedkin may well have convinced himself that they contributed to the film's ideological message, showing how the glories of the Soviet present were at threat from drunken tractor drivers, saboteurs and villains. Like the precarious equilibrium between the real and the unreal, however, Medvedkin's careful balance between satire and celebration can easily be unsettled – and unsettling.

Reception

Medvedkin's first feature was eagerly anticipated, and appeared regularly in published updates of films in production. He worked with typical speed and efficiency: in a table published in *Kino* detailing the costs of forthcoming productions, *Happiness* appeared remarkably cheap. In comparison to Dovzhenko's *The Far East* [Dal'nii Voskok, 1935, later to become *Aerograd*], for example, estimated at one million roubles, Medvedkin's film was costed at a mere 350,000.[46]

His timing was unfortunate, however. At the end of 1934 the debate on comedy, always complex, took a new turn. *Happiness* was released shortly after Alexandrov's musical comedy *The Happy Fellows* [Veselye rebiata, 1934], which was hailed by the influential administrator Boris Shumiatsky as a solution to the sticky problem of Soviet comedy.[47] The film united the three qualities that Shumiatsky proclaimed as essential in the new cinema of the 1930s (ideology [*ideinost*], joy [*radost'*] and merriness [*bodrost'*]), encouraging in the spectator a joyful appreciation of the Soviet world.[48] A light-hearted musical, drawing on the traditions of *estrada* (light music) and circus, *The Happy Fellows* represented, in many ways, a comedy directly opposed to that of Medvedkin, and a rejection of satire. Where Medvedkin sought laughter 'with a lash', Alexandrov offered merry laughter. As such, he answered the demands of the new climate. Medvedkin's comedy could not – indeed, did not want to – conform to those criteria.

Medvedkin's use of folklore was similarly out of step with the mainstream. At that famous Congress of Writers in August 1934, at which Socialist Realism was adopted, Maxim Gorky spoke of a literature that would be 'socialist in form but popular [*narodnyi*] in content'. This formula, which eventually became one of the foundations of Socialist Realism, seemed to pave the way for a reappropriation of folklore to the needs of the time: popular folk forms could be enlisted as valuable means of communicating with a mass audience.[49] The Vasiliev brothers' *Chapaev* of 1934, for example, which was much praised as pointing a way forward for Soviet cinema, pictured its hero in terms reminiscent of the hero of a folk epic, with unbounded courage and personal dynamism. Despite this thematic echo, however, the film's aesthetic corresponded broadly to Socialist Realism's call for simple stories, clearly told, that would communicate the supposed truths of socialism to a mass audience. Medvedkin's stylised folklore was markedly different – and more troubling.

Medvedkin was disappointed by the reception of *Happiness*, which was not shown 'on premier screens'. The central cinematic bureaucracy was, he claimed, hostile towards it.[50] Certainly, the reception of the film was ambiguous. In February 1935 *Kino* published two pre-release reviews of the film, both of which were largely complimentary.[51] Both essays, however, observed that the pre-Revolutionary sections of the film were more successful than those set in the modern age. The transformation of Khmyr from labouring peasant before the Revolution into a layabout 'idler' in the collective farm seemed unjust to the heritage and mentality of the peasantry, and the film (like Medvedkin's earliest satires) lacked a sufficiently positive hero.

This cannot have been a surprise to Medvedkin: at a pre-production discussion of the scenario the same doubts had been raised.[52] Then, he had promised to 'inject warmth' into his characters, and make it clear that Khmyr was a positive hero.[53] In practice, however, it seems that his subtly parodic vision of the modern world was not enough to satisfy the authorities. The stylised aesthetics of the film, rooted in the director's dream of a new kind of satire, were out of place in the culture of 'merriness' that the authorities were encouraging. Even more fundamentally, the film's ostensible satire on the peasant's 'misplaced' dream of individual wealth and 'happiness' was perceived by some to be fundamentally ambiguous, and thus potentially dangerous in the rapidly consolidating ideological climate of the mid-1930s. Thus it was with *Happiness* that the complexities of Medvedkin's relationship with authority took hold. And the sheer brilliance of this extraordinary film went largely unnoticed until some thirty years later.

4. *The Accursed Force*:
A Cursed Film

This was a time of change in Soviet cinema. In January 1935, two months before the ill-fated release of *Happiness*, the first All-Union Conference of Workers in Soviet Cinema heralded the emergence of a new period in Soviet cinematography.[1] Later that year Shumiatsky published an influential 'blue-print' for future films entitled *A Cinema for the Millions*, in which he called for a new, optimistic cinema.[2] The challenge for the film-maker was to work out what this meant in practice.

For Medvedkin, this was a difficult year. In this uncertain climate, the fate of *Happiness* was a source of great disappointment for him. Still, as he recalled later, 'I did not give in, and I poured my grief into work on a new screenplay'.[3] There was still, he believed, an urgent need for a film that would tackle the socio-political problem of the countryside under collectivisation from a broad historical perspective.[4] His next project, *The Accursed Force*, would do just that; it would be a story of 'the tragic fate of the Russian peasantry'.[5] By the end of the year costumes, set and actors were already in place, and production was about to begin, when GUK put a stop to proceedings.[6] Medvedkin could not have chosen a worse year in which to release one controversial film and plan another.

The Accursed Force is the missing chapter in Medvedkin's creative history. Reading the extant screenplays, one feels that this film may represent the apogee of its creator's imaginative fantasy.[7] It was to be an extraordinarily densely packed collage of folkloric archetypes, proverbs, ironic jokes and song, incorporating images of heaven, hell and everything in between. In a sense, these screenplays are Medvedkin's testament – the most important documents we have of the scale of his imagination, of his playfulness. They are also evidence of his ambition. For *The Accursed Force* is a film that tackles the really big questions: religion, freedom, and the meaning of life. It was, in Medvedkin's words, to be a film 'about the fate of the whole people [*naroda*]'.[8] And the director continued to struggle for its realisation until the very last years of his life.

*   *   *

The ideas for the new film developed out of the work that Medvedkin had done for *Happiness*, and in particular out of the successful pre-Revolutionary sections of that film. As he later explained, 'From that feast of ideas I had a great deal in reserve'.[9] The new film, however, was much more ambitious. The 'search for happiness' that had structured the first part of the earlier film was here given grander, more philosophical scope: it became the search of the Russian peasantry not just for happiness but for the very space of happiness – for their 'blessed lot' (*svetlaia dolia*). Medvedkin recalled:

> I decided to show that there was no place in Russia for the peasant [*muzhik*], for the peasant on the land. It was a satirical paradox: how could there be no place for the lord of the land? But it turned out that there wasn't, and that's how I developed the structure of a new comedy, a new philosophical comedy that I called *The Accursed Force*. The 'accursed force' was the peasantry, a gigantic force...[10]

Medvedkin's ambition in this film was to find an answer to the question that continued to vex film practitioners of the period: how to represent rural life. In reality, after all, the peasantry was something of a problem; with its traditional ways of life, it was resistant to the rapid and often brutal changes of collectivisation. In symbolic terms, however, it was the supposed backbone of the new socialism, the 'mass' force of Soviet Russia. In *Happiness*, Medvedkin had been accused of presenting an insufficiently positive picture of the collectivised countryside. His response, in *The Accursed Force*, would be to concentrate on the safer pre-Revolutionary context, on serfdom as a philosophical basis for a discussion of the peasantry – and of Russian history – in the abstract.

The film was to be structured around two parallel narratives. The first was a classic folkloric tale of the adventures of Ivan, youngest son of the merchant Vakula (and another version of Medvedkin's favourite Ivan the Fool). On his deathbed, the merchant divides his estate among his children: Mitrodor is given a smithy and Nikita a horse and plough. Ivan, the youngest son, is given nothing but a riddle: he is told to seek and find the 'accursed force', for it will enrich his life.[11] He sets off on a journey, meets and falls in love with the angelic Maria the Fair, and, after a series of adventures and encounters, is able to secure her hand. A fool he may be, but, in the time-honoured tradition of such heroes, he still gets the girl.

Ivan's story intersected with the film's other, philosophically more central, narrative. Maria the Fair is the daughter of old Saveli, leader of a tribe of peasants known as the Korezhinsty, who live in 'the wooden kingdom' under the oppressive rule of the evil Prince Obolt Obolduev. Obolduev is determined to put an end to the 'carefree' Korezhintsy's merrymaking – in particular, to their singing, which he sees as an explicit challenge to his rule, a spontaneous expression of peasant freedom. At the beginning of the film the Korezhintsy have no desire for freedom from their master, but they are forced by his cruelty into undertaking an epic journey, seeking a space in which they can live, sing and be happy. The quest takes them far and wide, to heaven and hell, before resulting in a spontaneous revolt against the evil prince, which will implicitly leave them liberated and able to build their peasant paradise on earth. The mass (the 'accursed force') becomes an epic hero, rejecting the repression of autocracy (the prince) and Orthodoxy (having experienced and rejected heaven and hell) at once.

The Narod

Medvedkin claimed that the film was 'based on motifs' from Nikolai Nekrasov's long poem 'Who can live well in Russia' ['Komu na Rusi zhit' khorosho', 1863–1878]. Nekrasov, radical poet and critic, had written his epic as a critique of the social and political situation in Russia after the emancipation of the serfs in 1861.[12] Like *The Accursed Force*, it is structured around a journey. Seven men meet, and ask themselves an impossible question: 'Who can live happily and freely in Russia?' Unable to agree, they set off across the territory to seek the answer.

Medvedkin evidently read Nekrasov's poem during April 1935, and noted what he perceived as its 'main points' – the 'soul' of the peasantry, and the idea of 'revolt' (*bunt*).[13] More directly, he discovered the seeds of his own narrative: one episode in Nekrasov's poem features an old man named Saveli, a former rebel who recalls his days as leader of the Korezhintsy people, deep in the forest far from the oppression of lords and rulers. In the text, this story of peasant freedom is merely part of a larger collage; for his film, however, Medvedkin chose to make it into the central plot, imagining the full story of Saveli's rebellious tribe and transposing it into his characteristically stylised world of fairy tale.[14]

The Korezhintsy's path to political consciousness is the central narrative in the film; escaping the legacy of serfdom, they are 'raised', in Medvedkin's words, 'to the level of future collective farm workers'.[15] Representing the peasantry as a whole, this oppressed tribe is 'a colossal potential force' (the 'accursed force' of the film's title), which has been 'oppressed and dehumanised by socio-economic conditions'.[16] At the beginning of the film the Korezhintsy are submissive – even passive. When the heroic highwayman Vaska Churkin (a Russian, more malevolent, Robin Hood, and a familiar figure from popular culture) kills their despotic Lord Obolduev, offering them liberty, they are horrified.[17] Unable to imagine life without a master, they are not yet ready for freedom, and they summon their friendly witch to revive the dead prince; she arrives on her broomstick and casts a spell, and the evil lord comes back to life.

At this stage, the Korezhintsy are distinguished by their ability to endure. Although passive, this endurance is a form of strength for, in the words of Saveli, 'Every lord, however evil he is, will necessarily die, but the people [narod] never dies. The narod is immortal. It is trampled, beaten, oppressed, but it lives and grows like an epic hero.' Here, Medvedkin tapped into a central trope of early Bolshevik ideology. While acknowledging the historical degradation and suffering of the peasantry, the discourse of 'immortality' offered a crucial validation of the mass. Maxim Gorky, in his influential speech to the 1934 Congress of Writers (usually seen as the beginning of Socialist Realism), had pronounced: 'The collective body is in some way distinguishable by a consciousness of its own immortality.'[18] The power of the peasant, worn down by suffering, lay in patience; his time would come, and he had to wait for his 'blessed lot'.[19]

An Earthly Paradise?

For all its virtue, however, such passive patience was a hindrance in a Revolutionary context, and the submissive peasantry needed to be remade as the politically active mass. The film's narrative, therefore, reveals that the peasant's 'blessed lot' is not necessarily given; it has to be seized. And, like the Bolshevik Revolution, it involves a rejection of all that has gone before.

The Korezhintsy's path to consciousness takes the form of a real journey. Escaping their master, their aim is simple: to find a place where they can toil for their livelihoods, work the earth, and create a kind of living paradise. 'There is a happy land,' Saveli explains. 'The quiet Don [River] flows through it. Men live like people there. They eat cakes on holidays...'[20] Elsewhere, in a song that was to provide a refrain throughout the film, the 'blessed land' appears as one of taverns, of mountains of wheat, of plentiful cooking pots, and of magnificent harvests.[21] This is the philosophical centre of the film. In Happiness Medvedkin had satirised what he called the peasant's 'dream of a well-fed life'; here he examines a more fundamental myth – that of the peasant's 'promised land'. In this film, however, his satire is careful, for it strikes at the heart of the Revolutionary ideal, which he has no wish to destroy.

In practice, the Korezhintsy discover that their 'blessed lot' is not so easy to find, and they are soon tired and disillusioned, with nowhere to go – a clear allegory of what Medvedkin described as the peasant's lack of a place in the world. Despairing of the earth, they head first to heaven and then to hell, on a literalised journey through the myths and images of popular religion. These scenes provide some of the most striking images in the screenplay; Medvedkin planned to use the full force of his satirical imagination to show that neither space, in the end, had anything to offer the honest peasant. His paradise, we understand, must be on earth.[22]

In line with the prescribed atheism of Bolshevik Russia, Medvedkin pictures heaven (complete with 'heavenly birds' and singing saints) as a lifeless space of monotonous virtue, in which the lusty Korezhintsy have no place. Hungry, they surround a heavenly apple tree and shake it; golden apples fall onto their heads but they turn out to be too hard to eat, and a metaphor comes to life: the fruits of heaven are, quite literally, unpalatable for these children of the earth. Driven to action, the peasants uproot a number of trees, harness a 'heavenly' white horse and begin to plough; after all, they say, 'How blessed can an unploughed land be?' Medvedkin's message is clear: the paradise that the Korezhintsy seek is one of virtuous labour, not the 'pointless' land that they have found.

Disappointed with paradise, we head to its apparent opposite: to the underworld. Here, as Medvedkin wrote in his screenplay, 'In contrast to the lifeless Heaven… there was an unbelievable commotion'. Emaciated devils rush around, carrying out their devilish service, stoking the flames of fires, etc. In an ironic nod to Russian folk superstition, Medvedkin's hell is rather like a giant bathhouse (the Russian *bania* – a cross between steam room and sauna, and a national institution).[23] It is hot and exhausting, with little air, but it is also a space of pleasure and plenty: its demons are the exhausted but obedient servants of the human sinner.[24] And, with its promise of indolent gratification, it has nothing to offer the Korezhintsy.

Thus the peasants' pilgrimage ends with a rejection of both heaven and hell. The film was to enact a *reductio ad absurdum* of religion: hell was a bathhouse that could be entered via a hole in the ground; Heaven was boring, demons obstreperous and foolish, and God just a bloke you meet on the street. God, indeed, was re-envisaged as something of a second-hand car salesman, implicitly so distressed by the low take-up of his product (heaven) that he's become a travelling salesman, offering free passes (*zapisky*) to anyone who'll take them. 'Don't I have to die first?' one character enquires, understandably. 'No,' he is told: just 'head west and keep right' (exploiting the double meaning of 'right' [*pravo*]).[25]

This down-to-earth deity was not a purely satirical figure, however. It was part of Medvedkin's understanding of the nature of traditional peasant belief systems. As Gorky had suggested, in that influential speech of 1934, 'God, in the conception of primitive man, was not an abstract concept, a fantastic being, but a real personage'.[26] According to Gorky, peasant religion was instinctively practical and pragmatic, rooted in the earth (a deity 'armed with some implement of labour') and in labour. It was this, he suggested, that could be the salvation of the peasantry – and even of Russia. The task of socialist art was to harness that realism, that putative love of labour, to the Revolutionary cause. As such, the Korezhintsy's search for an earthly paradise, a space of honest labour, was fundamental to Medvedkin's Revolutionary message.

A Stylised World

It is clear that Medvedkin was aware of the pitfalls of making another film about the 'collective-farm subject'; and he was concerned to present his picture of the peasantry within ideologically approved frameworks. Remembering the criticisms of *Happiness*, where the positive transformation of Anna and Khmyr into model members of the collective farm was perceived to have been less successful than the grotesque fantasies of the pre-Revolutionary sections, he was anxious to ensure that *The Accursed Force* avoided such failings. In particular, he emphasised that he sought to tell a positive story: in a convoluted echo of Shumyatsky's call for optimism in *Cinema for the Millions*, Medvedkin stated that '*The Accursed Force* must show the optimistic-tragic position of the peasant serf'.[27]

What was needed, Medvedkin believed, was a new way of representing rural life. 'The peasants of the last century, their huts, the soot, the dirt, the black wood, the oppression,' he wrote; '…all this seems principally to predispose one to show the horrors of the village, to dark, gloomy colours.' Friedrich Ermler's *The Peasants* [Krestiane, 1935], for example, had taken precisely this 'realistic' approach to the representation of the (contemporary) village. 'We are going about it in a different way,' Medvedkin claimed. 'Our peasants will be shining. They will be in homespun shirts and trousers. Blond, blue-eyed.'[28]

These words seem to link Medvedkin with the emergent genre of what might be called the Stalinist 'pastoral'.[29] The representation of the collective farm as a rural idyll became increasingly common in the second half of the 1930s (in stark contrast to the often difficult reality of agricultural life under collectivisation), reaching its apogee towards the end of the decade. In fact, however, Medvedkin's peculiar poetics would have produced a very idiosyncratic vision of the idealised rural space. As he noted in his diary, the film was to be based on 'Fairy tale. Paradox. Hyperbole.'[30] Like *Happiness*, it would blend a stylised picture of early peasant life with the fantastic world of folklore.

This was essential: the style of the film was part of its subject. For *The Accursed Force* was not only *about* the peasantry and its naïve belief systems, it was an attempt to visualise them. The world of *The Accursed Force* is a visualisation of a complete moral universe, peopled by figures from folklore, religion and mythology, all interacting and equal within the diegetic space of the film. As such, Medvedkin pictured what is often described as the 'dual belief' of the Russian people, in which pagan rites and myths interact with Orthodox ones, folklore with scripture.[31] In the filmscript, proverbs, metaphors and superstitions alike assume disconcertingly real form.

In the world of *The Accursed Force*, Medvedkin made no pretence of realism; the visual structures of the film were explicitly symbolic. Like the first part of *Happiness*, it was to be shot entirely in a studio, with 'artificial light, on artificially constructed sets'.[32] In line with its folkloric heritage, *The Accursed Force* deals in moral absolutes, and those moral absolutes were to be expressed visually in the film. Developing the expressive contrasts of black and white that he had used in *Happiness*, Medvedkin anticipated that the Korezhintsy would be light and 'shining'; black would be used only rarely, and 'for contrast'. In addition, Medvedkin planned to exploit the growing technology of colour cinema as part of his highly stylised meaning system, bringing his folkloric cinema closer to the brightly coloured and stylised images of the *lubok*. Maria the Fair, for example, is first pictured in a colour sequence singing in a meadow of multicoloured 'happy' flowers. Medvedkin intended that all the footage relating to her growing romantic relations with Ivan, together with the sequences of heaven and hell, would be shot in colour.[33]

This emphasis on light and colour was crucial to the film's ideological conformity. Medvedkin was well aware that he was walking a precarious tightrope between the optimistic and the tragic, the idyllic and the grotesque, in this highly stylised 'epic' of pre-Revolutionary serfdom. Perhaps responding to the criticism of *Happiness*, Medvedkin wrote that 'we want to rid this film completely of sombre, dark, expressionist features'.[34] This was particularly important in a film that sought to debunk and demystify the superstitions and myths of popular religion. As Medvedkin explained, 'If, for example, he [the cameraman, a role to be played by Igor Gelein] were to darken the set, it would immediately give the impression of mysticism'.

Like folklore, *The Accursed Force* is set out of time, in an unspecific premodern, rural Russia, and expected frameworks of time and space are challenged. As Ivan sets off on his archetypal journey, for example, he 'walks and he walks', and we do not know how far, or for how long. Shortly afterwards, he reaches the 'edge' of the world: a yawning blue void, into which he falls.

He lands, as if by magic, in the 'wooden kingdom' (that is, the world of the Korezhintsy), and it is there that he sees and falls in love with the miraculous Maria the Fair, granddaughter of Saveli. Such devices facilitate Medvedkin's episodic narrative, and enable the two stories to interconnect. But they are also part of the idiosyncratic vision of the world that is so central to the film. Distance is meaningless; the world is constructed vertically, almost as a series of layers, between which characters can move. Like the space of folklore, it is a space constructed according to events, and encounters, rather than according to geography. It is explicitly symbolic: heaven and hell are accessible by gate and manhole respectively – a literal realisation of the heavenly paradise (above) and 'the underworld' (below).

In the scenes of heaven in particular, we have a sense of how Medvedkin's extraordinary visual imagination might have worked. It is a cornucopia of cultural mythology brought to life: 'In Heaven,' he wrote in the screenplay, 'Heavenly birds sang...Heavenly apples grew.' The legendary twin birds Sirin and Alkonost (featured in Russian mediaeval texts, feminine and with beautiful faces and sweet voices) sing melodiously in the trees.[35] Saints and 'righteous men' stand in grassy glades and pray, intoning a single, monotone note ('a-a-a-a-a-a'), and familiar figures from Russian folk myth and religion (the saints Demian and Kozma, Maria of Egypt) wander around and chat. These sequences (which Medvedkin proposed would also be shot in colour – in shades of pink and blue, perhaps?) exhibit the characteristic excess of the director's fantasy. But they are not without satiric sharpness, as comedy shades into metaphor. The saints, for example, are described as motionless, with black faces, 'somehow chipped, like old icons'. They are symbols (literally, the iconography of religion) brought to life. As such, they represent ossification: the resistance of religion to the vitality of human life. The impression given by their immobility and by their discordant song, he writes, is one of 'unbearable grief'.[36]

The Lyrical and the Coarse

In addition to its overarching fantasy, *The Accursed Force* was to have a consistent level of more straightforward comedy. It was to be based on what Medvedkin described as the contrast of 'the lyrical and the coarse'.[37] In one scene, for example, Ivan is asleep under a crooked pine tree (echoes, we imagine, of the extraordinarily graphic shapes of crooked trees in *Happiness*) when he hears a distant whistle, and awakens to see the Korezhintsy flying through the sky 'like a flock of rooks' (exploiting the visual contrasts of the black and white medium). They land rather gracelessly, tumbling into trees, bushes and bog; a chaos of limbs, a flying collage of miscellaneous body parts, gradually resolves itself into human forms.[38] Even in written form, this is an extraordinarily graphic scene; imagined in terms of the striking two-dimensional techniques that Medvedkin had developed in *Happiness*, it becomes remarkable – lyrical, whimsical, and evidence of the apogee of stylised cinema that Medvedkin might have reached had this film been made.

Elsewhere, Medvedkin's comic gaze was more 'coarse'. Prince Obolduev, in particular, was to feel the full force of his satire. In one scene, for example, he is visited by a group that Medvedkin calls 'parasites' or 'shirkers' (*tuneiadtsy*). This motley crew – whose aim is to live off the labours of others, off the beleaguered peasant – is reminiscent of the horrifying array of caricatures in *Happiness*, who visit Khmyr as he builds his coffin. The roll-call is familiar: a fat deacon, two flirtatious nuns (perhaps to be naked again, as in *Happiness*, beneath their see-through habits?) and a bureaucrat. They provide a continuing level of slapstick humour in the screenplay. When their serfs (the Korezhintsy) disappear they have to fend for themselves, and they are, of course, incapable of doing so; there are hilarious episodes that show them in comic scrapes with cows and geese, attempting to find food. By the end of the film they have become quite wild, and are chasing the fat deacon with the firm intention of eating him.[39]

Rebellion

In the final sequences of the film, Obolduev – unable to survive without his peasants – begs them to return to work for him, promising that he will no longer forbid their song. Just as they are about to accept, he makes a fundamental mistake; he commands them to sing – and to sing for him. This is the turning point of the film. Saveli bows, and responds firmly: 'The head of the peasant belongs to the Tsar, his back – to his lord, but his holy soul belongs to the peasant himself, and you cannot command it.'[40] Song, then, plays a vital part in the philosophical structure of the film. It is, implicitly, the peasants' soul, the one thing that no lord can control; and it is the seed of the Korezhinsty's final rebellion.[41] As the prince in frustrated anger shoots into the crowd, we hear the sound of Cossacks in the distance; trees shake, and the fire and music of peasant revolt begin. Saveli sends the young Ivan and Maria away with the portentous words: 'Now our hour has come. Many will die here. But you save yourselves in the forest…and tell your children and grandchildren that the heroic people [*narod-bogatyr*] is immortal, and when it awakes and rises up, then its blessed lot will be found!'[42] As the Cossacks arrive the highwayman Churkin whistles, and Obolduev is drowned.

With his vision of the Korezhintsy's instinctual uprising against their lord, Medvedkin wrote himself into a larger debate on the nature of revolution that had run through the 1920s and into the early 1930s: the opposition between reason/consciousness (*mysl'*) and intuition/instinct (*chuvstvo* or *stikhiinost'*).[43] The question was an important one: should the Bolshevik 'Revolution' be understood only in terms of the rational, pseudo-scientific precepts of Marxist dialectical materialism, which seemed intrinsically Western in origin, or could it be part of a more organically Russian, instinctual, popular tradition of revolt (*bunt*)? Boris Pilniak's novel of 1922, *The Naked Year*, for example, had sought to conceptualise the Bolshevik Revolution as a 'spontaneous' popular uprising, an extension of Russia's instinctive peasant anarchy, a kind of 'people's revolt'.[44]

In the 1930s, however, this notion of Revolutionary anarchy was increasingly problematic for a state faced with the pragmatic need to build a viable, stable society. Thus, as Katerina Clark has suggested, the narratives of Socialist Realism were an attempt to reconcile these apparently opposing visions of Revolution.[45] Through the concept of 're-education', charting a 'path to consciousness' by which the spontaneous, instinctively rebellious energy of the hero was channelled into more focused, conscious Revolutionary commitment, they offered a domesticated version of earlier visions of mass energy. In the phenomenally successful *Chapaev*, for example, we witness just such a process, as the instinctively brave warrior Chapaev is exposed to the wisdom of a Bolshevik ideologue. In the literary text that became the model for such 're-education', Ostrovsky's *How the Steel was Tempered* (1932–1934), Pavel Korchagin is transformed, by participation in the Civil War, from violent but good-hearted hooligan into self-abnegating, rational hero of the cause. Thus, implicitly, the wild rebelliousness of the *narod* was to be harnessed as a force for revolution.

Despite Medvedkin's apparent attempt at conformity, therefore, in its focus on the mass and on visions of popular revolt *The Accursed Force* stood outside the consolidating trends of the 1930s. For the path of the Korezhintsy is not a path to real consciousness but, rather, an unleashing of spontaneous, Revolutionary energy. Impossible as it is to categorise, the film's remarkable blend of folkloric archetypes with Revolutionary tropes (the 'mass' and 'collective'), seems to echo early Revolutionary texts, such as Vladimir Mayakovsky's reworking of the biblical story of Noah's ark, *Mystery-Bouffe*, and Eisenstein's early Revolutionary films such as *The Strike* [1924], in which the collective body was the principal focus. As such *The Accursed Force* trod a dangerous line in 1936. In its vision of a despot overthrown, moreover, it might have been read as a challenge to the increasingly centralised power of Stalin's administration.

A Doomed Project

Medvedkin's timing could not have been worse. As production began on the film, changes were afoot in the Soviet political world. In June 1935 new central decrees were issued to increase control over the dissemination of 'counter-Revolutionary' literature, and the head of the NKVD, Nikolai Yezhov, assumed increasing power in the course of 1935–1936.[46] These were the years that saw the beginnings of the 'great purges' that took place towards the end of the decade. The first show trial of former members of the Bolshevik elite, Grigori Zinoviev and Lev Kamenev, took place in Moscow in August 1936, and by the end of the year political arrests were commonplace. The darkest years of the Stalinist 'terror' had begun.

In this climate of fear and uncertainty, it is scarcely surprising that *The Accursed Force* fell foul of GUK censorship. Officials in cultural spheres, uncertain of the tide of Party opinion, attempted to anticipate the correct ideological line. For all his apparent and long-standing commitment to the cause, Medvedkin, with his characteristic irony and irreverent humour, must have seemed far too risky a cause to promote.

The film was not without support, however. Medvedkin's archive contains a copy of notes by Eisenstein towards a speech about *The Accursed Force*, in which he states unambiguously that 'We understand, esteem and love Medvedkin'.[47] Eisenstein was evidently perplexed by what he described as the 'persecution' of Medvedkin, claiming not to understand the problematic reception of his satire. He offered a double defence of the younger director. First, Medvedkin's satire in *The Accursed Force* was safely targeted at a pre-Revolutionary, or even archaic, world. Second, his exaggerated, stylised aesthetic was not fantastical for its own sake but used its fantasy and exaggeration to make social statements. The master's words were not enough, however; *The Accursed Force* was never made, although Medvedkin did not cease to fight for it, producing at least fourteen versions of the screenplay between 1935 and his death in 1989. Today, *The Accursed Force* is a vital part of Medvedkin's legacy. Its lurking presence is a poignant reminder of the compromises that his survival entailed, the failure of his political dreams, and the gaping hole at the centre of his creative life. In a diary entry written in Paris in 1977 we find the phrase 'I want *The Accursed Force*!'[48] In notes towards an autobiography, Medvedkin marked *The Accursed Force* as one of the motivating ambitions of his life: 'For fifty years I did not tire of fighting for the production of *The Accursed Force*.'[49]

So, *The Accursed Force* remains one of the legendary unfinished stories of Soviet cinema. 'Such is the fate of my works,' Medvedkin wrote; 'they don't get onto the screen quickly, but nor do they disappear entirely.'[50] The screenplays are tantalising. In this unmade film we see, more clearly than anywhere else, the director's awareness of how images, myths and symbols shape dreams and desires. His subject, in this and – ultimately – in all his films, was the image itself. Medvedkin was profoundly and uniquely aware of the power of the symbol – doubtless the legacy of his early years as a propaganda officer; this awareness inflects all his work, and is the source of the playful irony that saturates his cinematic world.

5. The Miracle Worker

In the difficult and dangerous climate of 1936 Medvedkin urgently needed to reposition himself, and in an article published in August of that year, he announced that his next film would be a complete 'revision' of his previous work: 'The screenplay for *The Miracle Worker*, written after *The Accursed Force*, represents an act of profound artistic self-reconstruction. I recognise the total impossibility of using the experience of any of my previous works in this new production.'[1]

This public act of renunciation must have been a difficult one. Medvedkin's work to date represented a single mission: the search for a form of political satire; this was a reluctant rejection of that search. *The Miracle Worker* was made at a time when his relationship with the regime was at its most fraught. It is a key transitional work, produced as a response to the failure of his most cherished project, *The Accursed Force*, and signalling the beginning of the end of its director's active career in satire.

As the Second Five-Year Plan entered its third year, Medvedkin was working with appropriate efficiency: *The Miracle Worker* was premiered in February 1937, only seven or eight months after filming began (and around a year after work ceased on *The Accursed Force*). It was, Medvedkin proclaimed, a 'realistic' film, a move away from the 'stylisation' of his early works. As such, it focused on a contemporary subject, on the idea of 'socialist competition' with which Medvedkin had had direct contact during his year on the film-train. In contrast to *The Accursed Force*'s dangerous archaism, this film was squarely located within the Soviet Russia of the 1930s.

So, in the film's opening sequences, we encounter a successful farm, 'Dawn of Victory', the most productive milk-producing collective in the region of the river Oka, in central Russia (Figure 10). A neighbouring collective, 'White

10. The opening shot (*The Miracle Worker*, 1937)

Sands', enters into 'competition' with Dawn of Victory. It stands little chance of success, however, for it is hindered by old and intransigent members of the community, including the rather ferocious old milkmaid Varvara.

The heroine of the film is the young Zinka (played by Zinaida Bokareva, a child radio star, whose extraordinarily high-pitched and melodious voice is one of the film's most striking qualities). She is the fourteen-year-old grand-daughter of the head of the collective, Matvei, and her dream is to become a milkmaid. Zinka secretly teaches herself to milk the collective's herd, with remarkable results. She makes friends with the cows, treats them with kindness, and for her they produce an apparently boundless yield. Zinka's success is soon the talk of the region, and her 'lesson' is taught to the whole collective. Varvara undergoes a dramatic transformation, and it is eventually she who manages to produce a record-breaking milk yield (Figure 11). Thus the White Sands collective secures the banner of victory from the vanquished Dawn of Victory, and Zinka is invited to Moscow to speak in honour of her achievement.

In parallel with this sociological plot the film offers a romantic narrative, between Zinka and a young shepherd called Ivan, who achieves renown as a hero when he rescues the community's cattle from a chance fire. Zinka falls immediately in love with him, but the relationship falters; carried away by his own glory, Ivan is reduced to boastful wonder at his achievements, and Zinka tires of his self-obsession. It is only as she is heading to Moscow for her unforgettable encounter with Comrade Stalin that they are reconciled, and the film's love narrative offers a resolution to parallel the principal glory of productivity. The two are united, ultimately, by their service to the state.

Life Has Become More Joyous...

This was a difficult time, as directors struggled to negotiate the political mine-field, to interpret the changing paradigms of Socialist Realism. As Medvedkin well knew, the pitfalls encountered were particularly evident in the 'collective-farm subject'. *The Miracle Worker* was released in the same year that work on Eisenstein's *Bezhin Meadow* [Bezhin lug] was stopped, for the second time, by order of Shumiatsky. Like *The Miracle Worker*, *Bezhin Meadow* was to focus on the 'socialist reconstruction of the countryside'. It too treated the 'generational conflict' – the idea of radical youth pitted against a reactionary older generation. Based on the famous story of young Pavlik Morozov, who had denounced his retrograde father to the state, the film was accused of 'direct slander against our Russian countryside'.[2] Eisenstein was criticised for depicting the transformation of the countryside as 'the pathos of elemental destruction', rather than as organised development brought about by class struggle.

In *The Accursed Force*, Medvedkin too had been interested in elemental struggle, in a vision of peasant rebellion that dealt in the moral polarities of good and evil that Shumiatsky criticised in *Bezhin Meadow*. In the Soviet Union of the mid-1930s, however, there was no place for such dangerous anarchism, and the suppression of *Bezhin Meadow* indicated a growing unease with the rhetoric of Utopianism and revolt. The chaotic forces of Revolutionary energy were to be transformed into the compliant virtues of a pragmatically viable social order; the revolting peasant was to be transformed into the happy collective-farm worker.

Although Medvedkin claimed, at the time and in retrospect, that *The Miracle Worker* was an attempt to conform to the prevailing aesthetic, in fact the film is far more complex than that might suggest. In the shift between his two projects of 1935–1937, *The Accursed Force* and *The Miracle Worker*, we can trace the director's changing relationship with the political imperatives of his time. In his notebooks, notes and ideas for the two films appear side by side, even interwoven. As early as June 1935 he wrote that 'Socialist competition would be a good theme for a film'; on another page, we find a newspaper cutting featuring a prize-winning cow called Witch, the name eventually used for the starring beast of *The Miracle Worker*.[3]

As always, however, Medvedkin's interest lay not only in political reality but also in its slogans. In this same notebook, he scribbled: 'Life has become more joyous [*zhit' stalo veselee* – a Stalinist catchphrase], and when life is more joyous, work goes better…' This fragment may offer us a key to the film's genesis: in *The Miracle Worker*, Medvedkin engages with contemporary reality at the level of its rhetoric. Alongside its apparent concern with contemporary issues, the film offers a metatextual reading of the question of 'representation', of the terms in which the Soviet village *could* be pictured. It is, in a sense, a sustained reflection on the discourse of 'happiness' that pervaded 1930s culture; from the director whose 'laughter with a lash' had been criticised for insufficient optimism came a film that gently – almost imperceptibly – parodies that very ideal.

The Russian Village: Landscape and Song

Medvedkin's ostensible turn towards 'reality' in this film was signalled by a key shift: from filming in studio, as was planned for *The Accursed Force*, to filming on location.[4] *The Miracle Worker* was shot on the Kirov Collective Farm in the village of Fediakino, in the Moscow region, and Medvedkin boasted of working directly with real members of the community. Local milkmaids taught the actresses to milk; one newspaper announced: 'Zinka milked six cows today!'[5] All this was a pointed rejoinder to the criticisms of Medvedkin's previous 'stylisation', and to demands that he engage with the reality of agricultural transformation.

In practice, however, Medvedkin clearly understood that Socialist 'Realism' had little to do with reality 'as it was', and more to do with how *it should be*. Film-makers were called upon to represent the present in all its shining achievement, whether or not that achievement was yet there in reality. Thus, *The Miracle Worker* represented the collectivised countryside as an idealised pastoral. In contrast to films such as *Earth*, *The General Line* and, more recently, Ermler's *The Peasants*, all of which pictured the countryside in difficult transition, in this film the collective farm is represented as a dream almost realised (the 'idyll becoming reality', as one critic enthused).[6] In parallel, the landscape, ravaged by collectivisation and industrialisation, is transformed into a nurturing earth in which man and nature work harmoniously together.

The Miracle Worker is a film explicitly concerned with landscape and, working with the cinematographer Igor Gelein (who was to have filmed *The Accursed Force*), he discovered a new visual code, using cinematic devices that scarcely figure in his earlier work. In contrast to the relative absence of 'views' in the stylised, two-dimensional space of *Happiness*, this film is often dramatically three-dimensional, abounding in richly framed panoramas that evoke the vastness of its 'boundless' Russian landscape. In Medvedkin's words: 'the horizontal of the meadow, the waves of the hills. Here meadows cannot be encompassed by the eye and far off, on the horizon, the watery expanses lose themselves in mist.'[7] To create this impression of distance and depth the landscape sequences rely on wide-angle shots, and the breadth, or 'horizontality', of the landscape is conveyed through long tracking shots. In the film's opening sequence, for example, we see a close-up of a birch tree copse, and hear women singing in the distance (Figure 10); gradually the singers approach the stationary camera through the trees, and then the camera follows them as they move, and a vast and majestic panorama of river and horizon opens up behind them. Finally, the camera leaves the women behind, and offers a long pan of the empty landscape.

One reviewer praised Gelein for giving this filmed picture of the Russian landscape a 'diverse and painterly aspect', and it is certainly true that the visual codes of this film echo those of landscape painting.[8] This was a conscious strategy: Medvedkin based his vision of the Oka and its meadows on the painted landscapes of Isaak Levitan, a member of the group of late nineteenth-century artists known as the Wanderers. 'Whatever I do,' he wrote in the screenplay, 'I can't convey the richness of its [the Russian landscape's] beauties better than Levitan.'[9] This painterly intertext marked the landscape of *The Miracle Worker* as archetypally Russian. The river Oka, Medvedkin suggested, was an 'older sister' of the Volga, 'the main highway of Russia',[10] and the film overall had to be a 'clearly Russian national film'.[11] Its pastoral Russianness, however, was very different from the folkloric poetics of his early work.

Absent in *Happiness*, in *The Miracle Worker* nature is almost fetished. Zinka is often surrounded by flowers; the river acts as a silver pool in which trees, reeds and gentle hills are reflected. This 'lyrical and romantic' vision reaches its apogee in the scene of harvest: 'There are no better days on the Oka than the haymaking days,' Medvedkin enthused in his description of the film, 'when the meadow is transformed into a bright, multicoloured carnival.'[12] In the filmed version (the black and white film tinted to give the impression of colour, and to distinguish this sequence from the rest of the film), we encounter the same rhythmically scything figures that were later to populate the landscapes of Pyrev's iconic *Cossacks of the Kuban* [Kubanskie kazaki, 1949], produced some thirteen years after *The Miracle Worker*. Compositionally, these frames exemplify the landscape aesthetics that structure the film: they appear to be almost self-consciously pastoral, positioning the human body within a visual canvas in which man and nature fuse. One shot, picturing women creating hay bales at evenly spaced points across a field, seems to echo the choreographed sequences of a good Busby Berkeley musical, as the women's bodies move in apparently organic harmony.

After the bumper harvest is accomplished, the peasants gather on the river-bank, their faces lit by the glow of a camp-fire, to sing folk songs. *The Miracle Worker* was Medvedkin's first realised sound film, and, just as song was to have played a crucial role in *The Accursed Force*, so here music and singing have a diegetic function. From the opening sequence on, folk choral harmonies provide a vital backdrop to the film's evocation of an 'eternal' Russian landscape. As Medvedkin described it: 'From the high bank, across a birch glade, milkmaids come down for their break. They walk and sweetly sing their girlish song...In the hot June midday sun the river seems to doze, and the song sounds far and wide across its vast expanses.'[13] Thus song, often heard in the distance, provides a means through which the depth and breadth of the landscape is articulated. Throughout the film, changes of scene are marked by the repetition of images of the river, its water meadows, and the horizon. Accompanied by song, these scenes form choral interludes, creating pauses in the pace of the film, and ensuring that the implicitly timeless spirit of rural Russia and its landscapes forms the backdrop against which the contemporary rhythms of collectivisation are viewed.

In *The Accursed Force*, peasant song was to have been Revolutionary – part of the assertion of freedom and revolt that was the film's focus. In this film, by contrast, an important shift in its thematic role took place. Instead of insurgence, it symbolised rural harmony and contentment, and linked the collectivised village to traditional and implicitly unique ideals of Russianness. Medvedkin used the famous Piatnitsky vocal ensemble to provide the music for the film. Banned during the First Five-Year Plan, this long-standing choir had been criticised for promoting traditional village life. Its revival in the mid-1930s was part of a broader revival of folk culture, and the creation of the village as pastoral idyll. So, Medvedkin seemed to fall into line; the village, he wrote, was a more 'authentic' space than the city, and its culture – its song in particular – more 'Russian'.[14]

Tenderness: An Ordinary Miracle

According to an enthusiastic contemporary review of the film by Nikolai Klado, *The Miracle Worker* offered 'a new screened vision of the Russian village'.[15] The use of folk choral music in a film about collectivisation was not new, however. In 1934 Igor Savchenko had produced *The Accordion* [Garmon', 1934], in which, as Medvedkin remarked in notes towards his own film, 'People don't speak, they sing'.[16] In Savchenko's self-proclaimed 'musical comedy', one of the first examples of the 'Stalinist pastoral', music was thematic ('the accordion is the poetry of the Soviet village,' a voice-over announced): most significant dialogue was sung, and village life was represented in overtly stylised terms as a round-the-clock song and dance routine. In this film, music provided the focus around which another debate on 'joyousness' was centred: the film's hero, Timoshka, is much loved in his village for his music. Made 'secretary' of the collective's rural council, Timoshka vows to renounce music for the sake of ideology, thus leaving the villagers bored, idle and unhappy, and at the mercy of kulak saboteurs, who try to lure them with their own brand of music. In the end, Timoshka fights an ideological battle not with the pen but with the accordion; he realises that the Soviet village must be merry, and wins back the villagers with his music and dance.

In *The Accordion*, the classic struggle between old and new – between Timoshka the heroic accordion player and jealous 'kulaks' – remained. In *The Miracle Worker*, such struggles are muted. As Klado recognised, the organising principle of the film is 'peacefulness'[17] – the battles of the five-year plans and of collectivisation are transmuted into the benign rhythms of nature. In addition to its value in describing the style of the film, Klado's emphasis on 'peacefulness' hints at the thematic preoccupations of *The Miracle Worker*. The film's principle 'miracle worker' is Zinka, and her revolution in working practice is driven by an unusual quality: tenderness.

As the film begins, the White Sands collective is saddled with a herd of recalcitrant and disobliging cows, which produce little or no milk. The bovine company, indeed, provides much of the comedy in the film. Its heroine is Witch, described by the vet as a 'a former cow' (*byvshaia korova*), in ironic reference to Stalin's category of 'former people' (see Chapter 3). The burly Varvara engages in pitched battles with Witch (in once scene, angered by her aggressive approach to milking, the cow-heroine drags the old woman into the river). By contrast, young Zinka transforms the recalcitrant beasts into hero(in)es of Soviet production.

In contrast to Varvara's aggression, Zinka has a Revolutionary method: she talks to Witch as to a person. And so she is able to milk the 'former cow', proving that she has life – and milk – still in her. So great is Zinka's affinity with the creature, in fact, that Witch will come to her call. The young girl takes a register of each cow by name, discovering their particular needs and quirks: poor Zaraza (whose name means 'Pest') is 'puny, dirty, thin, unhappy', and initially too ashamed to show her face, but Zinka renames her Little Siren [Sirenka]. The beast is so moved by her own transformation that a tear of joy trickles from her vast brown eye.

Implicitly then, by regaining her femininity the cow regains its role in the collective. This transformation is echoed at a broader level in the transformation of old Varvara. Like the cows Witch and Pest, Varvara has lost her femininity – she cannot access the 'tenderness' (*nezhnost*') that, according to Zinka, is the secret of successful milking. In one key scene, Zinka attacks the older woman, accusing her of having dirty hands that hurt the cows, of being insufficiently 'tender'. 'You have a masculine voice, rough hands,' she protests; 'you need to learn to sing.' Varvara's reaction is revealing: these are the hands that have built the 'New World', she counters, not the delicate hands of the bourgeoisie.

Varvara is a woman of strife – one who has fought for the 'new [Soviet] world', but who has also retained vestiges of the superstition that characterised the 'old' world: despairing of Witch, she calls on the village sorceress for help. Through Varvara, Medvedkin explores the shifting social balance between older Revolutionaries and the new generation of Soviet citizens (like Zinka), born under Bolshevik power and now coming to maturity in the mid-1930s. She is out of place in the Soviet Union of the 1930s. As one reviewer described it in 1937, she 'cannot find in herself the warmth, the love, that are necessary in labour today'.[18] Like that of her nation, her life has been a difficult one. 'I need tender words…' she muses; 'but I have never said them to anyone…I have barked all my life…and caressed my husband only with black words.'

She too is eventually touched by the miracle of tenderness, however. In a scene that is self-consciously magical in appearance, Varvara is pictured by

11. Varvara – the transformation (*The Miracle Worker*, 1937)

moonlight, by a stream, beginning to wash her hands (Figure 11). As Medvedkin suggested in his pre-production article about the film, the task of the director here was to make Varvara's transformation 'beautiful and memorable'.[19] So, as she cleanses herself, implicitly recapturing her softer self, the landscape seems to echo her transformation; this is the film's most extended panoramic sequence, a hymn to the natural glories of the river. Thus Varvara is tied to an organic, natural vision of Russianness – she becomes a kind of Mother Russia for the new world. The (necessary) violence of revolution gives way to the nurturing tenderness of nature.

In the end, therefore, it is significant that it is not Zinka but Varvara who breaks the milk production record – persuading Witch, now a prize-winning 'record breaker', to produce a magnificent fifty-seven litres in a single session. And this double transformation (of cow and woman) is brought about by Zinka, and her cult of kindness. Later, as the delegates proudly ride to Dawn of Victory to announce their record-breaking production, Varvara finds her singing voice; as the choral harmonies surround her, her 'masculine' voice discovers its feminine melodies and we see her, alone, singing the folk songs of her past. The transformation is complete.

A Feminised Revolution

Thus opposing visions of revolution are played out in the representation of different categories of femininity. The femininity of the cows – ever more fertile in the regime of tenderness, producing the milk that will, implicitly, nurture the nation – is a comically absurd microcosm of the film's broader message. It is no accident that Medvedkin uses a female choir to provide the musical score for the film. The narrative, too, focuses predominantly on women – on Zinka and Varvara in particular. Matvei and Ivan are almost lone males in an essential feminine collective. In addition, the star of the Dawn of Victory, Maliutka (her name is a diminutive of the word 'small' [*malaia*], ironically chosen, Medvedkin wrote in the screenplay, for the actress's 'impressive height and magnificent proportions'),[20] is feminine – choked with emotion as she relinquishes her cherished banner to the victorious White Sands delegates.

In these terms, Medvedkin represented his 'generational conflict'. Zinka and Maliutka are children of this new world; the un-tender Varvara, by contrast, represents the older generation, for whom struggle predominated over 'tenderness', femininity being sacrificed to the cause. The realised Utopia of the 1930s, however, called for new forms of behaviour. The 're-education' of Varvara, a version of a common trope in Socialist Realist narratives, is thus transformed into an almost magical re-feminising – as if Khmyr's formidable wife Anna, in *Happiness*, were suddenly to exchange her admirable 'tough love' for a more feminised Revolutionary consciousness. In place of the Utopian vision of revolt, we find a curiously muted Revolutionary philosophy of kindness.

The novelty of this tender revolution can be seen in comparison with *The General Line*. Eisenstein's film shows the transformation and modernisation of the village in terms of mechanisation; for Medvedkin, it is achieved by simple kindness. The humble equipment of White Sands is able to vanquish the technological majesty of Dawn of Victory through the application of that formerly underappreciated Revolutionary quality: tenderness. The cows in Eisenstein's film are scraggy inhabitants of a mechanised world; in Medvedkin's film they are the plump, record-breaking providers of the nation's food. The harshness of revolution gives way to a vision of plenty. Varvara scrubs off the dirt – metaphorical and actual – of Revolutionary struggle, and is reborn into the sanitised idyll of Stalinist Russia.

The Unforgettable Encounter

The thematic significance of emotion extends to the film's climax. Maliutka's tearful speech echoes the joy of the final scene, when Zinka appears in the Kremlin palace. Arriving on the podium to collect her prize, facing Stalin

12. The Unforgettable Encounter (*The Miracle Worker*, 1937)

himself (Medvedkin cut real documentary footage of Stalin into the film, ensuring a 'real' image of the great leader [Figure 12]), she is overcome by emotion, unable to deliver her speech, and asks the kindly presiding official for permission to 'weep from great joy'. That permission granted, however, she finds that so profound is her joy that 'Somehow I can't cry!' In the screen-play these words marked the film's ending, as Zinka was 'accompanied from the tribune by an ovation'.

In the film's final version, however, her failure to cry gives way to a speech; her wordless subscription to the values of her nation is transformed into a speech of conformity, of adulation of the great leader Stalin. The reasons for this shift are not known. Perhaps Zinka's inarticulate conformity proved somehow subversive – it risked destabilising the all-important happy ending that marked the film's subscription to the demands of Socialist Realism. Giving Zinka words, Medvedkin wrote her in to an emergent tradition of articulate women, symbolic daughters of the great Father Stalin. Stalin's Russia was full, it seems, of weeping daughters: in Zarkhi and Kheifits' *Member of the Government* [Chlen pravitel'stva, 1939] a similarly emotional Liubov Orlova addresses her public address to the Father. In Chiaureli's 1949 *Fall of Berlin* the heroine exhibits an adulation for the great leader that is part romantic, part childlike. As in these later films, in *The Miracle Worker* the trajectory to Moscow provides the triumphant summit of the film: in contrast to the chaos of Khmyr's visit to the city in *Happiness*, Zinka's trip to Moscow is a success.

Exaggeration

Although, with its romanticised images of landscape, an aesthetic of tenderness dominates *The Miracle Worker*, it is clear from Medvedkin's notes on the film that he had not abandoned his roots. 'The whole thing has to be built on trans-formation,' he wrote in his early notes; 'hyperbole, poetic language, paradox.'[21] Attempting to avoid the political pitfalls of his former work, Medvedkin hoped to capture the 'idyll, in the process of becoming reality' through a careful balance between contemporary reality and elements of the fairy tale. 'Zinka is a realistic figure,' the director asserted, 'and she remains real even in the episodes with eccentric consequences.'[22] Zinka, then, would provide the film's stability, and answer the demands of the authorities for a 'positive hero'. With that assured, Medvedkin felt able to revel in his characteristic hyperbole.

And revel he did. From the opening credits on (the film's title, set against a background of stylised flowers, to the accompaniment of folk music), the dominant mode of the film is that of exaggeration. *The Miracle Worker* is a film saturated with self-consciousness – far more stylistically playful, in a sense, than *Happiness*.

As in all Medvedkin's work, style carries meaning, and here the metaphor of tenderness pervades the film's very poetics. The pastoral idyll is overtly, excessively, romanticised. In its lush plenty, the landscape of *The Miracle Worker* is as stylised as the bare landscapes of *Happiness*. And Medvedkin openly indulges this extreme lyricism, part of the film's thematic emphasis on that 'feminised' revolution. This sense of stylistic excess gives the film a parodic twist, as if Medvedkin mocks his own pastoral idyll even as he revels in it. In one memorable incident, some English tourists take a pleasure boat cruise down the Oka during harvest; surrounded by the extraordinary landscape, they ignore it and doze. In ironic reference to Russia's long-standing discourse of national uniqueness (the Russian 'soul'), the boat's captain implies that the landscape is too beautiful and too soulful to be appreciated by the cold, 'indifferent' hearts of capitalist Westerners.

The director's pervasive irony is particularly evident in the film's love narrative, where the 'magical, eternal beauty' of the landscape provides the setting for romance between Zinka and Ivan. 'Here we rediscover the pastoral idylls that have been forgotten in our day,' Medvedkin wrote, 'when the world was decorated by guileless heroes, the shepherd and the shepherdess.'[23] His tongue firmly in his cheek, Medvedkin pictures his young heroes on the river-bank, framed by the eternal beauties of their world: 'And now, as if vanquishing centuries, on the banks of a Russian river, traces of the long forgotten history of our ancestors have been revived...'

This epic tone allows Medvedkin to explore changing categories of heroism. Our first encounter with Ivan is with 'a very young, long-legged boy', sitting beneath a tree and dreaming of heroism. 'I'm ordinary, my duties are ordinary...' he admits; 'but I want something extraordinary...' Zinka's grandfather Matvei, having decided that she is too young to fulfil her dream of becoming a milkmaid, decrees that she is to be a lowly 'under-shepherd', and takes her to work with Ivan. The shepherd is immediately enthralled by the young beauty, who informs him in no uncertain terms that 'I want my young man to be a hero'. Ivan, coincidentally, wants to be just that: 'I want the whole world to find out about me, and for that I'm ready to throw myself into fire or water!' And ('as in a fairy-tale') what should appear but a fire in the collective's cattle shed? Ivan runs to the rescue and becomes a local – and national – hero, winning the love of Zinka.

From the beginning, Ivan's heroic deed is framed in comic terms. As the cattle shed burns, we see a somewhat dissolute and disorganised fire brigade, attempting to respond to the emergency call. Cross-cut with the hysterical energy of Ivan's feat of rescue, they move extraordinarily slowly towards the fire, arriving long after the shed has collapsed into embers, and with Ivan lying unconscious from exhaustion. With comic equanimity, the firemen get out their cigarettes and use a still-glowing ember to provide a light. Here, the backing music is sharply differentiated from the languorous folk harmonies of the rest of the film, typical rather of the piano tunes used to accompany silent film comedy. The scene lacks dialogue, operating according to the laws and techniques of silent cinema, and contributing to Medvedkin's playful collage of cinematic cliché. In plans for this scene in May 1936, it was positioned under an explicit heading: 'Chaplin'.[24]

Thus Ivan's heroism is framed by Chaplinesque comedy. With Medvedkin's characteristic irreverence, his dreams of trial by fire and water are brought graphically down to earth, made literal, as he plunges himself repeatedly into barrels of water before running in and out of the blaze (Figure 13). The contemporary critic Oleg Kovalov suggests that Medvedkin here parodies the emerging categories of heroism in Socialist Realist culture: 'The film mocks the hero of propaganda, who does not drown in water and does not burn in fire.'[25] Ivan is an epic hero of the modern age; so heroic, indeed, that he manages to rescue nineteen calves, although the collective has only eighteen of them! As such, he *overfulfils* his heroic quota – just as collective farms and factories were called upon to overfulfil their production quotas.

In Ivan, we see a slogan brought to life: an ordinary man becomes a superman. Here Medvedkin engages with the shifting cultural myths of the

13. Ivan the hero (*The Miracle Worker*, 1937)

age. In *The Accursed Force* the collective was hero; here the heroes are two young individuals, Zinka and Vania, and their social ascendance is mapped onto their love story. Yet things do not run smoothly. Vania deals badly with his own heroism. Zinka initially loves him for his bravery ('You are ... extraordinary!' she says quietly); the problem, however, is that he loves himself for it. He is bemused and fascinated by his own glory. 'I became greater [*vyshe* – higher] than myself,' he exclaims, wonderingly (and repeatedly), echoing the words of the popular 'Aviators' March' ('Higher still and higher'), which became an anthem of the period, a metaphor of national excellence in all fields. And, in the recounting of his tale, he uses ever greater exaggeration: 'I broke through a lock this thick!' he boasts, brandishing a vast chunk of metal that increases in size with every telling.

Our down-to-earth heroine, busy with her own 'miracle' of milking, has little truck with Ivan's self-obsession, and their love founders. Thus Medvedkin undermines the Socialist Realist fairy tale later epitomised in Alexandrov's 1940 film *The Radiant Path* [Svetlyi put, 1941], when the heroine's ascent in social terms – her success as a member of the labour collective – is rewarded by romantic success. Here heroism does not guarantee happiness; it is goodness and simplicity that are rewarded. Although Zinka and Ivan are reconciled at the end of the film, and the film thus conforms to more stereotyped romantic endings, this is despite, rather than because of, his status as a 'hero'.

With Ivan, Medvedkin drew on his folkloric roots. Like Khmyr in *Happiness*, he is another version of the Ivan the Fool prototype (in Medvedkin's words, an 'unsuccessful hero', whose exploits are often comic and whose naïvety is paramount, but whose goodness wins through in the end). A semi-literate shepherd, he is, in Zinka's trenchant description, 'not the brightest, but good'. Proudly reading out the newspaper articles that tell of his extraordinary feat, we are struck by the way he mispronounces basic words. He is, Medvedkin seems to suggest, not equipped to understand the political slogans within which his instinctive bravery has been framed, an ordinary boy thrown into a new world, seeking to understand himself through new criteria: 'When I got glory, I lost myself,' he confesses. And it is not his instinctive bravery but his basic goodness that is his final salvation.[26]

Miracles

The subversion of categories of heroism evident in the figure of Ivan is part of the film's broader enquiry into the nature of 'magic' and miracles – as Jay Leyda suggests, the film can be read as a series of 'variations on the theme of magic'.[27] Ivan (having summoned and vanquished fire) becomes convinced he has miraculous powers. Alone by the river, experimenting with his own enchantment, he wishes a corncrake to croak – and it does; he wants to see the moon – and it appears. But the magic fails him at crucial moments: 'I want Zinka!' he cries; but she does not appear. The scene is one of high romance; Vania is a solitary romantic hero, Zinka is his love, but the romantic denouement is postponed, and the hero is something of a fool.

In this way, magic is brought down to earth. The miracles in which the film deals are ordinary miracles, the achievements of real people. By contrast, real sorcery yields nothing – as we discover when, despairing of Witch's milk yield, Varvara calls on 'the last sorceress' of the region for help. The sorceress in question resembles the crone of *Happiness* (eventually so unable to find her place in the new world that she attempted to hang herself on the windmill), and as such her intrusion into the pastoral 'realism' of the film makes a striking contrast: a candle is placed on top of the cow, and she begins to weave her spells, circling around the bemused and indifferent animal. Her extraordinary incantation, which evokes the pharaohs and gods of ancient Egypt (and is comically interrupted by her demands for money from the beleaguered Varvara), is eventually cut short by the revolt of the cow itself. As Medvedkin described it, 'Witch gets fed up with this shamanism', lifts the witch up with her horns and sends her running terrified up a tree, followed swiftly by Varvara herself. The two old women sit, in Medvedkin's words 'like crows', on the branch of a familiar, bent, dead tree (Figure 14).

14. Varvara and the sorceress threatened by the cow Witch (*The Miracle Worker*, 1937)

Here, then, we rediscover the stylised, laconic landscapes of *Happiness*: a dead tree, an empty set, and a strikingly white background, against which the crow-like shapes of the two women are thrown into relief. In this film, however, this two-dimensional space takes on a further layer of meaning: it is a symbol of backwardness. The movement between three-dimensional ('realistic') space and folkloric space creates meaning. Characters who inhabit the stylised space are implicitly those who remain in the past: Varvara, for example, is pictured in a barren landscape with a crooked and leafless tree in the early sequences of the film. Zinka and Ivan, by contrast, are shown in a more organic relation to space, and Zinka in particular reveals an innate affinity with the natural world, represented by the pastoral landscapes that so often frame her. In parallel, Varvara's later conversion to 'tenderness' is linked to nature.

This contrast of old and new worlds is overt in a later scene, where the sorceress is pictured trying to cast a spell that will make a cow produce cream, rather than mere milk. She has put felt boots on the cow's feet (black on the front, white on the back), and makes it walk around her in a circle as she casts her spell. A young boy watches the performance, providing a commentary that makes explicit the thematic battle between old and new. 'You're the only thing left from the old world,' he says; 'they've remade the whole world, but they can't do anything about you...!' Her threatening reply – 'I'll survive into the shining future' – is undercut when, symbolically, her spells produce only sour milk. Thus the thematic point is underlined by poetics. While Zinka begins to break records in milk production the sorceress remains trapped in her stylised world, within the enclosing circles of magic and superstition. Hers is a world without views, without an outward perspective; it is symbolically left outside the pastoral lyric that surrounds the forward-looking members of the community. While their milk is fresh and bountiful, hers is scarce and sour.

The Travelling Barber

As Varvara and the sorceress cling desperately to their tree, they are discovered by one of the film's most appealing characters – the travelling barber, Savva. A kind of Soviet Don Quixote (Medvedkin's creative notebooks are dotted with references to Cervantes' hero, and it seems likely that this was an explicit reference in the creation of the figure of Savva),[28] he trots around the country-side on his be-hatted donkey, visiting local communities to offer his services. His system is ingenious: the donkey carries mirror and tools, so that they can set up shop anywhere (Figure 15); the unruly beast has a comic tendency to wander off at inopportune moments, however, leaving barber and client stranded.

Earlier in the film, we have seen Savva so absorbed in reading aloud from his newspaper that he doesn't notice that his donkey has left the path and is carrying him in circles around a tiny twisted tree. The image is a familiar one: in the symbolic space of *Happiness*, the endless circles of the runaway tractor were a symbol of backwardness, a pointed counter to the straight lines (the linear trajectory) of progress. Here, too, Savva's eccentricity, his foolishness, is comically evident in his failure to notice the donkey's wilful disobedience, and Varvara mocks him ruthlessly. The situation is more complex, however, for his distraction has a worthy cause. Throughout the film, the newspaper is a symbol of Savva's quirky modernity. He is, as Ivan announces admiringly, an 'ideological [*ideinyi*] barber', bringing news as well as hairdressing to the communities that he serves. It is he, for example, who informs the community of Zinka's invitation to Moscow (bursting rowdily into the expectant and reverent silence of the villagers as they wait for news of Varvara's record-breaking milk yield), and he who knowledgeably informs his clients that beards are outmoded in Soviet Russia.

Although he is a comic figure, therefore, Medvedkin intended that 'the eccentricity of Savva [would] be kept within the bounds of the real world in which he works'.[29] Medvedkin described Savva as 'the image of new Soviet

15. Savva the travelling barber, shaving Ivan (*The Miracle Worker*, 1937)

man', whose virtue lies in the pride he takes in his 'labour'.[30] He is inordinately proud of his status as 'regional' barber, and proclaims the value of his craft: 'personal hygiene is a matter of state significance'. Through Savva, Medvedkin allows modernity to enter the world of *The Miracle Worker*; but it does so within a comically absurd framework. His political expertise, his knowledge of the Comintern (the organisation responsible for maintaining links with communist parties abroad), for example, is oddly and pointedly out of place in the lyrical landscape of this corner of old Russia. As he reads aloud from his newspaper, the jargon of Soviet-speak, in which he obviously delights, is absurdly discordant against the timeless backdrop of the film.

Excess

Savva is at once modern and folkloric, comic and serious. He moves between the film's diverse stylistic codes, between the idealised pastoral and the comic absurd, from folkloric stylisation to Chaplinesque eccentricity. At one level, we can read these shifting poetics as symbolic, where the folkloric (the world of the sorceress) represents backwardness, and the pastoral (that of the collective farm) is invested with the positive energy of the future. Such neat categorisation is tempting, and certainly revealing, but it does not work for Savva. More generally, it also fails to acknowledge the sheer *excess* of Medvedkin's playful and self-conscious exhibition of shifting style. Each style, or device, is exaggerated to a point of near-absurdity, and as such the film seems to be saturated with an ironic distance that inflects the spectator's experience and carries the film's basic meaning.

In part, this is provided by authorial intervention. In this, his first sound film, Medvedkin does not relinquish the extra-diegetic possibilities of the intertitle. His titles signal plot movement, introducing new episodes, but they also provide commentary. 'An extraordinary occurrence in the White Sands farm,' one proclaims; another adds, with an imagined wink, 'A girl's heart is not made of stone'. These titles maintain an authorial consciousness at the heart of the film, and keep the spectator at a distance from the film's action. The director was clearly determined to frustrate audience expectation and play with cinematic cliché; referring in the screenplay to an earlier scene he wrote gleefully that 'here, according to the laws of cinema, I should have a fight...' – and pointedly offered no such climax in the film.

In addition, despite the film's ostensible subscription to realistic aesthetics, Medvedkin's style often undercuts its own apparent verisimilitude. In one episode, for example, Zinka and Matvei travel by horse along the river bank, arguing about her future. The camera remains at a fixed, mid-range distance from them, creating an almost two-dimensional effect whereby we see only the profile of the galloping horse and its riders. This has the effect of de-familiarising the dialogue, refusing the characteristic shot-reverse-shot structures of narrative cinema. Instead of involvement in the debate, we are offered a comic experience, which Kovalov describes as 'almost cartoon'.

Thus, the pastoral idyll of *The Miracle Worker* must be seen within an ironic mode. At the very beginning of the film the excessively lush landscapes of the opening frames are followed by a curious comic episode, which exhibits the satiric sharpness of Medvedkin's early work and injects a crucial darker element into the film's 'optimistic' comedy. The White Sands delegates are taken on a tour of the competing collective, Dawn of Victory. One contemporary review described this scene as an unambiguous celebration of the joys of agricultural achievement.[31] As such, it surely missed Medvedkin's basic irony, for the lugubrious tour guide who walks the enthusiastic visitors around the farm presents a truly odd figure, lacking the enthusiasm that might be expected for her role, and appearing instead deeply bored, even depressed. Kovalov goes so far as to describe her as a 'robot'.[32]

In the screenplay, Medvedkin was explicit. 'The milkmaid tour guide is a strange character in the film. On her face there is grief, in her voice, indifference and disdain for everything living. But she has to boast and show her wares' (Figure 16). Thus the delegates are taken around the wonders of Dawn

16. The lugubrious tour guide (*The Miracle Worker*, 1937)

of Victory, and 'the more bored the guide seems to be, the more happily they exclaim'. As they come across Savva at work she boasts indifferently that 'We have our own barber', and her tone is exactly the same for him as it is for more grandiose 'sights', such as milk pasteurising equipment and production quotas.

The combination of the excessive excitement of the White Sands delegates with the sullenness of the tour guide is a send-up of what we might call 'agricultural tourism'. Such a 'tour' of the achievements of ordinary people and ordinary communities was a common feature of film 'newspapers', which comprised news fragments taken by different cameramen in different regions, emphasising the valuable contributions of the region to the great achievement of the state. In the words of Gorky, describing one such project, the newspapers should feature ordinary communities so that the 'little people' might know that 'their every labour is returned to them in the form of those achievements of which this journal tells'.[33] Medvedkin's gently parodic tour brings such 'achievements', and the very project 'socialist competition', down to earth ('we'd like a barber too!' Matvei and his associates enthuse...). And, with its peculiar discordance, it provides the lens through which the rest of the film is to be viewed.

A Sanitised Utopia

Deciding how to read this film presents a serious challenge to any student of Medvedkin's work. On the one hand, it is a clear call for a new stage of Revolutionary development: the White Sands collective is, implicitly, left behind – run by representatives of an earlier generation of Revolutionaries. Matvei, leader of the collective, was explicitly intended by Medvedkin to look like Mikhail Kalinin, a figure significant in the early years of Revolutionary socialism.[34] The future is represented not by his Revolutionary discipline, however, but by Zinka and Ivan's naïve but fervent 'tenderness'. Read in these terms, it is a weakly sanitised version of Medvedkin's earlier vision of the future ushered in by peasant/Bolshevik 'revolt'.

Thus, in the culture of the late 1930s, the call for 'tenderness' replaced the harsher messages towards which Medvedkin had strived in his early films. The satire was transformed into the 'lyric comedy' – a genre with which Medvedkin was never comfortable, but which was increasingly the only available comic form. As Shumiatsky said, 'The victorious class wants to laugh with joy. [...] the laughter in Gogol, Shchedrin and Chekhov is accusing laughter, laughter derived from bitterness and hatred...We believe that, if Gogol, Shchedrin and Chekhov were alive today, their laughter would in the Soviet Union acquire *joie de vivre*, optimism, and cheerfulness.'[35] Medvedkin seems to subscribe, then, to the call for cheerful, positive laughter. As one reviewer described it in early 1937, 'His previous habit, in laughing at something, was to denigrate. In *The Miracle Worker*, laughing, he affirms.'[36] In the words of another: 'For the first time the spectator can start to love the heroes of a Medvedkin film.'[37]

On the other hand, the film may be read as testament to its director's disillusion with the Utopian project of socialism that he had so eagerly embraced – a symbolic rejection of the central premises of Stalinist society. The film's thematic emphasis on cleansing, and on tenderness, might be read as an ironic jibe at the criticisms that Medvedkin had encountered for his work, a sly comment on the 'cleaning up' of Soviet reality that created the narratives of Socialist Realism. Here Medvedkin – who throughout his career had striven to create films that would be 'harsh', that would use satire to ridicule, to force change through shame – stylistically 'cleaned up'. Tenderness is not just the theme of the film but the basis of its very conception. The implicitly 'uncouth' stylised poetics of *Happiness* are transmuted into the 'tender' landscapes of *The Miracle Worker*. This, as the director testified, was in a sense an acknowledgement of failure – the failure of Medvedkin's cherished ambition to create an acceptable form of political satire. And the monotone, bored demonstration of the milkmaid guide reveals this sanitised Utopia to be a sadly diminished version of Medvedkin's dream of Soviet society.

Reception

Contemporary reviews of *The Miracle Worker* seem not to have noticed the apparent ironies and excesses of Medvedkin's style. The film was discussed at a forum organised by Mosfilm, by a group that included the directors Vsevolod Pudovkin, Evgeni Cherviakov, Boris Barnet and Alexander Macheret, together with the Hungarian critic and would-be director Béla Balázs, then living in Moscow.[38] The discussion was reportedly 'warm', and Medvedkin's 'sharp turn' towards a different aesthetic, his rejection of 'stylisation' in favour of 'reality', was praised. The film was not considered an unqualified success, however. Pudovkin accused it of poor acting and stilted and unsynchronised dialogue. According to Barnet, it lacked realistic detail: 'The collective farm workers are pictured outside their everyday life,' he complained; the real material conditions of life were not shown.

This criticism perhaps reveals more about Barnet himself than it does about Medvedkin; his 'everyday' comedies of the 1920s (*Girl with a Hatbox* [Devushka s korobkom, 1927] and *House on Trubnaia Square* [Dom na Trubnoi, 1929]) were remarkable for precisely the kind of 'characteristics of everyday life' that he felt were lacking in *The Miracle Worker*, showing characters enmeshed in the material reality of 1920s Moscow. In *The Miracle Worker*, by contrast, Medvedkin's hyperbolic stylisation demanded an *absence* of detail – his characteristic 'laconicism'. Similarly, the 'artificial' quality of the dialogue is pointed and cannot be accidental; from the very beginning, the contrast between Zinka's remarkably high pitch and Varvara's gruff, manly tones is part of the film's comedy – and its meaning.

Despite these criticisms, the film's unusual blend of the realistic with the stylised was noticed, and even praised, by the only two reviews of the film published in early 1937. Shevchenko, for example, claimed that *The Miracle Worker* was a genuine representation of folk aesthetics, rooted in 'living material', in contrast to the 'stylisation' of folklore that Medvedkin had offered in *Happiness*.[39] As such, it seemed to be in line with the emerging paradigm of the Soviet 'village' film. In general, however, the reception of the film can be described as lukewarm, and it occupies no place in the pantheon of Soviet film classics. It was viewed as a transitional work, part of the director's urgent project of re-education, and Medvedkin himself later described it as an unsuccessful attempt to 'sing "in a different voice"'.[40] According to Rostislav Iurenev, *The Miracle Worker* 'did not have the same audacity or sharpness' as *Happiness*.[41] In the words of Demin, 'here Medvedkin stopped being himself'.[42]

More recent critics have been kinder to *The Miracle Worker*. The American historian Jay Leyda, who first saw the film in 1971, described it as 'extraordinary': 'it is difficult to understand,' he wrote, 'why Soviet critics and historians have not taken the opportunity to draw attention to this extraordinary film. It was just as ahead of its times as *Happiness* was, and now that other films are beginning to catch up, it should be known the world over.'[43] Leyda went so far, in fact, as to claim *The Miracle Worker* to be superior to *Happiness*. 'The film is full of moments of beauty that the acid and biting tone of *Happiness* did not allow. And it is in that sense that *The Miracle Worker* is a better film, losing nothing of the satirical vigour that is Medvedkin's exceptional contribution to Soviet cinema.'

More recently still, but for different reasons, the critic and film-maker Kovalov has described *The Miracle Worker* as 'the most underestimated film in our cinema'.[44] He offers a provocative reading of the film as a subversive satire on the developing politics of the 1930s: '*Happiness* mocked not the flaws of collective farm construction, but [...] social mythology, the ideological foundation of tyranny.' This, Kovalov asserts, had been merely hinted at in *Happiness*, but became the structural principal of *The Miracle Worker*. The film's apparent conformity is in fact parody: it is 'a unique artistic organism – almost an encyclopaedia of the social mythology of the '30s'.[45]

It seems, then, that the fate of *The Miracle Worker* is to be read according to the political imperatives of the age: criticised in its time for failing to conform, and then in subsequent periods for that very conformity. Now, according to Kovalov, it is to be appropriated to a post-Soviet age as a curious pre-parody of *later* cultural norms. After all, although Alexandrov's *The Happy Guys* had appeared in 1934, *The Miracle Worker* was released a few months before Ivan Pyrev's *The Rich Bride* [Bogataia nevesta, 1937], and before the genre of socialist realist 'musical comedy' was consolidated. Thus, following Kovalov, the film is to be viewed as postmodern before its time, saturated with the kind of ironic distance that characterises a post-Soviet attitude towards Stalinist cultural mythology.

The task of the contemporary spectator is to balance these competing readings. Certainly, *The Miracle Worker* is an acutely self-conscious film, a sustained reflection on changing aesthetic norms, and Kovalov recognises Medvedkin's most distinctive quality: his acute awareness of social myth. He may, however, underestimate the complexity of Medvedkin's relationship with the regime and the culture that he served throughout his life. He is not easily appropriated to an anti-Soviet cause. Perhaps the film mocks not the 'ideological foundation of tyranny' but the complex and shifting paradigms of Sovietness, the search for a form through which to represent Soviet reality; and Medvedkin is as much part of that search as he is its critic.

6. New Moscow

After watching *The Miracle Worker* for the first time at the Moscow Film Festival in December 1971, Leyda ended his enthusiastic review of that film with a poignant question: 'What mixture of beauty and satire did the director achieve after 1936? Can we see it?'[1] The plea was pertinent: Medvedkin's third feature film, *New Moscow*, was banned before its first public screening – apparently for 'ideological' reasons. Accepted for distribution on 20 November 1938, the film was unexpectedly withdrawn in January 1939. It has still only rarely been screened in the West, and today remains almost as little known in Russia as elsewhere.

New Moscow was Medvedkin's last comic feature of this productive period – and almost the last of his career. Its failure signalled the final demise of the director's cherished dream of political satire. In an interview with Marcel Martin, Medvedkin described *The Miracle Worker* as 'a lyric comedy' and *New Moscow* as a 'happy' one.[2] For anyone familiar with the director's quest for 'attacking cinema' and 'sharp comedy', these terms are themselves revealing, indicating the director's reluctant capitulation to an alien aesthetic. After the poor reception of *Happiness*, the rejection of *The Accursed Force* and the muted acclaim of *The Miracle Worker*, it was important that the director continue along his 'new path'.

Again, Medvedkin took Soviet reality as his subject. This time, instead of the thorny topic of the collective farm he focused on the Moscow 'General Plan', a grand project for the reconstruction of the capital, announced by Lazar Kaganovich in 1935. The plot of the film is simple: a young engineer, Alexei (Alesha) Konopliannikov, works on a construction site in the furthest reaches of the Soviet Union ('three thousand miles from Moscow'). Building a hydro-electric power station by day, he and his comrades have, in their spare time, made a moving scale model of their beloved capital, Moscow. At the flick of a switch, it shows the city transformed from its former, pre-Revolutionary shape into the glorious future capital of the Soviet Union. They are invited to exhibit the model at the All-Union Agricultural Exhibition in the capital, and Alesha and his grandmother are entrusted with the task.

On his way to Moscow Alesha meets and falls in love with a young urban beauty named Zoia. He is waylaid, however, when he comes to the aid of another young woman, the swineherd Olia, whose prize piglet has escaped. After a frenzied chase, Alesha and Olia eventually capture the wayward piglet and are able to join Zoia in Moscow. Thereafter a love plot dominates the film. Zoia is as enamoured of Alesha as he of her, but she is also enthusiastically courted by a rather hapless young artist, Fedia. The four have a series of absurd adventures and misunderstandings, which eventually conclude in the happy resolution of two loves: the first between the 'serious' couple, Alesha and Zoia, and the second between the more obviously comic characters, Fedia and Olia. At the end of the film all look set to live happily ever after.

This romantic comedy takes place against the backdrop of the capital city in flux, and the transformation of Moscow provides the film's sub-plot, and its visual impact. Alesha's model is exhibited to a vast audience. Initially there is disaster: the film is run backwards, and instead of Moscow's glorious new buildings rising from the ashes of the old we see the glorious future of the capital collapsing into its past. The situation is put right, however, and the idealised vision of the capital is finally revealed, to rapturous applause. Thus the celebration of young love is accompanied by a celebration of the achievements of the state.

*   *   *

For Medvedkin, laughter (in its ideal, satirical, form) had always been a means of avoiding cliché, a way of standing outside the rapidly consolidating norms of Soviet cinema. As he announced in interview in 1985,

> I realised that these films, the usual sort depicting love, the good life and good positive people, were not for me. I think that a comedy that has some greater philosophical meaning will succeed, but the kind where Vania loves Tania or Tania loves Petia and so there's a triangle…I leave that kind of work to others, I do not believe that it's true to life.[3]

What, then, are we to make of *New Moscow* – a film that appears to be saturated by both cinematic and ideological cliché? The film's slapstick comedy sits alongside a love triangle (happily resolved – in the time-honoured tradition of Shakespeare's *A Midsummer Night's Dream* – in the form of two unions) and an ideological narrative of the transformation of Moscow. The result is a somewhat uncomfortable hybrid, but with memorable episodes that never-theless hint at the director's playful brilliance.

With *New Moscow*, Medvedkin tried to negotiate a new, safer, comic path, and the film seems at first glance to lack the conceptual sophistication of his early work. What it offers instead is a succession of 'attractions'. We see, for example, Alesha and Olia frantically chasing Olia's truant piglet Heinrich, trying to trap him inside a cylinder, only to find that he escapes through a hole in the centre, and they meet only one another as they approach from either end. Later, they disguise the selfsame piglet as a baby in order to smuggle him onto the city metro (Figure 17), where he snorts his way through the journey, his porcine nose protruding out of the swaddling and attracting the bemused attention of other passengers. A paediatrician travelling on the same metro takes a look at the evidently ill infant, and they fear discovery. The doctor, however, is merely disconcerted and pitying at Heinrich's remarkably ugly appearance – 'the poor child looks just like a pig...'

Many of the classic ingredients of farce – missed trains, mistaken identities, letters that should not be sent, etc. – are present in the film. In one long sequence, Fedia and Olia meet at a lido and inadvertently end up carrying

17. Alesha, Zoia and Olia with Heinrich on the metro (*New Moscow*, 1938)

one another's clothes, separately caught out in a rainstorm. Fedia, dressed only in a bathing suit, tries to steal clothes from a scarecrow; as a young couple approaches, looking for shelter from the rain, he disguises himself as that scarecrow and they cuddle at his feet. Later, Alesha and Zoia are so carried away by their first kiss that they allow their car to hurtle unheeded through the streets of the capital, spinning around Red Square in circles that echo the spinning of the couple's hearts.

Amidst this, traces of Medvedkin's grotesque imagination remain. Searching for Alesha at a carnival, Alesha's ageing grandmother is told that she has to wear a mask if she is to stay. She is thus transformed into what Medvedkin described in the screenplay as a 'dazzling blonde with a cheeky smile and an improbably turned-up nose'.[4] Indeed, so attractive does she become that she is seduced by a playful passer-by, who asks her to dance, but retreats in shock when informed: 'this blonde hasn't danced since the reign of Alexander III!' For the rest of the scene the grandmother's mask remains upside down on the back of her face, and Medvedkin ably exploits the grotesque comic potential of this inanely grinning face, inverted against her greying hair, in a disconcerting image that recalls the stylisation of his earlier films.

Such escapades are part of the film's succession of comic 'attractions'. For the most part, however, the film's comedy lacks the sharper edge of Medvedkin's satire. It lacks even the stylised exaggeration of *The Miracle Worker*. Alesha's grandmother (played by the eminent elderly actress Bliumental-Tamarina, a celebrated 'people's artist', who was seventy when the film was made), for example, fulfils a purely comic role. Fedia and Olia hover uncomfortably between the comic and the serious: they are neither as successfully stylised as comic characters in Medvedkin's earlier films nor as fully developed and three-dimensional as would be needed for a conventionally 'realist' narrative. In his attempt to create Alesha as a 'positive' hero, Medvedkin produces a two-dimensional character. Thus, although the film is certainly 'jolly', it does not have the stylised coherence of the director's earlier films. The real interest of *New Moscow* lies elsewhere – in particular in the director's sidelong glance at the Soviet Utopian project. It is in this, surely, that the reasons for the film's banning lie.

Centre and Periphery

As its name suggests, this is a film about Moscow. It is structured around a pivotal symbolic relationship between the capital and elsewhere, between centre and periphery.[5] Its opening scene is set at Alesha's construction site ('far from Moscow'), where former Muscovite engineers are building their hydroelectric power station, transforming marshland into habitable space.

These former city dwellers talk and sing of the capital reverently, with love and excitement. One man has his beloved beard shaved off, because 'they don't have beards in Moscow' (recalling Savva's firm insistence on the ideological appropriateness of a shaven chin in *The Miracle Worker*). This sets the tone for the rest of the film, where the capital's symbolic weight is consistently emphasised. During his train journey, for example, Alesha sings to the assembled passengers, joyfully reinforcing Moscow's status as Utopian destination: 'I will see my native capital...' While in the city he seeks to buy a radio, so that on his return he will still be able to hear the beloved 'voice' of his city.

Moscow, then, is firmly at the centre of the imaginary map of the nation, and this structural binary dictates the film's narrative. The central love story between Alesha and Zoia founders on a confrontation of centre and periphery. While Zoia wishes never to leave Moscow, Alesha will not stay: he is bound to return to where his work is needed. Briefly, he wavers, lured by the appeal of a metropolitan lifestyle. In the end, however, his social conscience wins out: his destiny lies at the periphery, at the front line of socialist construction. A happy ending is secured when Zoia packs sturdy 'swamp boots' (difficult to find in a Moscow department store) and heads off to follow Alesha 'to the end of the world'. The final scene returns us to our point of origin, a marshy construction site, now already transformed into a small Soviet town. As their comrades celebrate Alesha and Zoia's return, and their shared vow to work and live on the periphery, they sing of and to the city, raising toasts as if to an absent friend.

Although the protagonists finally dedicate their lives to the periphery, urban space is thematically and poetically central to *New Moscow*. On one level, the film is a glorification of the new capital, of the energy of reconstruction, the creation of a public space that is the pride and joy of the whole nation. The real-life General Plan for the reconstruction of Moscow, instigated by Stalin and Kaganovich in 1935, provides the subtext here: Alesha's 'living' moving model of Moscow functions as a *mise en abîme* of a Moscow that *really* moves, propelled into action by the force of transformation. On another, it takes a playful swipe at the fantastic ambition that underpinned the reconstruction of the city, picturing Moscow not as a grand public arena for the affirmation of citizenship but, rather, as a chaotic and fluid adventure space for its young protagonists.

Both visions of the city are reflected in stylistic choices. Where *The Miracle Worker* had begun a stylistic shift in Medvedkin's work away from the folkloric poetics of *Happiness* towards a partially more 'naturalistic' or three-dimensional style, *New Moscow* seems to complete the process. After a reading and discussion of the screenplay in May 1938, Nikolai Klado claimed that the director had 'finally moved away from the stylised manner and extreme hyperbole that was characteristic of his early works'.[6]

Superficially at least, *New Moscow* was narrative cinema, with an ostensibly realistic aesthetic. Its scenes of Moscow were largely shot on location. Thus, the arrival in Moscow of Alesha, his grandmother and Olia takes place within familiar urban settings, in the very centre of the city. The young people travel (with piglet) on the metro, recently completed and celebrated as a glorious achievement of Socialist might. Alesha's grandmother travels on a route that reveals the Bolshoi Theatre, the House of the Soviets and key central buildings. This, the area around the Kremlin, was the first part of the city to be renovated and transformed as part of the General Plan for the reconstruction of Moscow. It became the iconic symbol of the grand Soviet capital.

In the first scenes of the city, however, these spaces appear as much chaotic as monumental. Trolleybuses and pedestrians cross the frame, crowds jostle, creating a sense of metropolitan energy. This sets the tone for Medvedkin's cinematic city. Throughout the film, Moscow appears as a series of adventure spaces. Our protagonists travel by metro, drive the city's streets, visit its sites of leisure. Medvedkin's Moscow is fluid and chaotic, and as such, it recalls the 'everyday' (*bytovie*) films of the 1920s, such as Room's *Bed and Sofa* [1927], in which the city in flux was represented not as a monumental capital but, rather, as the lived space of ordinary citizens.[7]

Between 1930 and 1940, however, the status of Moscow as cinematic city had begun to shift. As in *The Miracle Worker*, the journey to Moscow became the celebratory finale of the classical Socialist Realist movie, a reward for spectacular labour achievement. Moscow, in such episodes, would appear as monumental symbolic space, the glorious capital of a glorious nation. In Alexandrov's 1938 *Volga Volga* the harmonious heroine Dunia composes a hymn of glory to the nation, and is invited to Moscow to perform. As her barge enters the capital, Moscow's grand embankments provide a majestic backdrop to her celebratory song.

This shift in the status of the city was echoed in a shift of cinematic style. In Mikhail Kaufman and Ilia Kopalin's *Moscow* [Moskva] of 1926, rapid montage created a vision of the city as fragmented and dynamic. In comparison, later documentaries such as Boris Nebylitsky's *Moscow* [Moskva, 1937] pictured the reconstructed capital as a stable, framed space. As early as 1936, in Alexandrov's *The Circus*, a newly monumental Moscow was represented by the symbolic spaces of Red Square and the Kremlin, framed by the window of the newly built and rather glamourous Hotel Moskva.

In Medvedkin's *New Moscow*, the opposition between these two ideas of urban space is made explicit, in both theme and style. Two opposing visions of public space coexist in the film. The first is the crowded lived space of contemporary Moscow in which our protagonists operate. The second is the relatively unpeopled, fantastical space of Alesha's model of the capital. And it is in the collision of these two visions of the city that the subversive force of the film can be found.

The City in Flux

The lived space of contemporary Moscow is dynamic and contingent, in the process of change. Medvedkin used studio sets to picture a city that 'really' moves, simulating the moving of apartment buildings and the collapse of landmarks. In one scene Fedia is trying to paint a scene of Moscow, but is unable to do so because the cityscape is changing before his eyes. Buildings are pulled down before he has a chance to 'fix' them in paint (Figure 18), and he is reduced to trying to capture 'the Moscow that is disappearing'. 'I only need two days,' he pleads, but the buildings move as he paints them. Another scene shows Alesha's grandmother visiting her sister at home when buildings suddenly begin to move outside the window. Panic ensues, but the situation is soon clarified: it is not the whole world, but merely their own block that is moving, lifted off its foundations and shifted a few metres to the side!

This apparent absurdity was rooted in the fantastic reality of the time. In 1937 work had begun on the reconstruction of old Tverskaia Street and its

18. The city changing before our eyes (*New Moscow*, 1938)

transformation into Gorky Street. This was to be the central artery of the 'New Moscow', a monumental parade avenue and pilgrimage route to Red Square. And it needed to be appropriately grand. Thus, during the building of Gorky Street, over fifty buildings were moved, allowing the street to be widened.[8] The publicity that these removals acquired was unprecedented. Indeed, the influence of Moscow's transformation was the basis of another comic film, *Make a Noise, Little Town* [Shumi gorodok, 1941], in which a provincial town decided to emulate the city's ambitious projects by moving its own buildings to improve public space; if the capital could do it, after all, then so could the periphery. Rhetorically at least, the power of Stalin's Russia was apparently unlimited: it could even remake the physical world. With his taste for excess and exaggeration, Medvedkin took such publicity at face value, and so the landscape of his cinematic city brought slogans alive.

Masquerade

Medvedkin pictures, then, the Moscow of the mid-1930s in all its chaotic and increasingly fantastic reality. But he also pictures the city as lived in. Indeed, at times this Moscow seems to be principally a city at play. While evidence of construction and labour is all around them, our protagonists seem to spend much of their time in the city's new leisure spaces, meeting in elegant riverside cafés, bathing in specially constructed lidos or dancing at carnivals. These are the principal spaces within which their comic adventures take place.

One important section of the film takes place on 'Carnival Night' – a title emblazoned in lights above the city skyline. Alesha heads to the carnival hoping to woo Zoia away from Fedia. His grandmother, from whom he has been separated since the ill-fated train journey, goes there to try to find him. Inevitably, chaos ensues. The masks and costume of carnival permit transgression, allowing for tricks and mistaken identity. Both Fedia and Alesha are dressed as white bears, so Zoia cannot tell her two suitors apart. Later, she incites one of her friends to don a mask and pretend to be her, luring away Fedia and enabling Zoia to frolic with Alesha.

The idea of carnival gave Medvedkin an alternative visual vocabulary through which to represent the city. In the working screenplay for *New Moscow* he described a scene that does not figure in the final film, and in which we can trace the director's abiding fascination with the mask, so memorably evident in the masked soldiers of *Happiness*. He describes how, in the 'soft summer twilight', citizens make their way through the streets of Moscow to the carnival: 'A trolleybus careers along a busy street, crammed full of masks. Out of its windows hang wolves' heads, harlequins, Chaplin, a white bear…'[9] The screenplay goes on to detail a highly visual montage of moving masks, a succession of shots, each of six to eight metres, with the evocative descrip-tion: 'Along the streets, singing songs, a group of jolly masks hurries to the carnival. [...] Singing masks pass the Moscow Kremlin...'

If fully realised, this sequence would have created a bizarre and striking picture of the city *en fête*. And although it does not appear in the finished film, the visual chaos of carnival does provide an alternative perspective on the spaces of the city. These are scenes of leisure and revelry, in which Medvedkin seems to take a purely cinematic pleasure. But they also serve a more important purpose. Medvedkin, as we know, was more than aware of the shifting poli-tical validity of folk culture and the ancient artistic models of the fairground and 'buffonade'. During the first decade after the Revolution street theatre and mass demonstrations had sought to exploit the structures of folk theatre, to be participatory and 'spontaneous', echoing Mikhail Bakhtin's much-exploited conception of 'carnival' (in literary genres), where the subversive, 'centrifugal' energy of popular entertainment threatens to overturn established hierarchies.[10] It is surely no accident that Bakhtin's concept emerged out of the Soviet context, in which questions of popular culture and mass festival carried par-ticular ideological weight.

This emphasis on iconoclasm had underpinned Medvedkin's focus on 'revolt' in *The Accursed Force*. In that film, it was the peasants' spontaneous song and dance that represented the first stage of their rebellion. By the late 1930s, however, this focus on spontaneity had all but evaporated, replaced by a growing emphasis on more structured public parade. The staging of icono-clasm had given way to the staging of conformity, as street demonstrations were transformed into the remarkably choreographed Red Square parades that later became emblematic of Soviet Russia.

Medvedkin's urban carnival, then, can be read as a pointedly reduced and sanitised version of his earlier ideal of 'revolt' and folk *bunt*. The device of carnival enables Medvedkin to retain elements of his beloved grotesque, but within a realistic mode. There is nothing iconoclastic about this display of urban leisure. Nor, indeed, is there a great deal of fantasy. If in *The Accursed Force* we would have seen 'real' bears (leaping from the forest to abduct Maria the Fair), in this film we see Alesha and Fedia in bear costumes. The fantastic cast of characters who would have peopled *The Accursed Force* are here reduced to mere disguise. Ultimately, the carnival forms part of the film's ostensibly 'realistic' picture of the Moscow of the 1930s. And, as such, it can be only a plaintive echo of the director's earlier fantasies.

The Fantasy City

Within that ostensible realism, however, the film offers a secondary picture of the city that is overtly idealised – surely even to the point of parody. This is the unpeopled space pictured in Alesha's model of the city. It acts as a simulacrum of a city that, as we have seen, is itself being transformed into fantasy.

In a climactic scene, Alesha and his partners are gathered to present their cinematic vision of the future capital to an assembled audience of dignitaries. A disaster occurs: the film is placed in the projector the wrong way, and in place of the glorious achievements of socialism rising from the ruins of old Moscow the audience sees these great buildings collapsing and old Moscow returning (Figure 19). These are some of the most memorable sequences of the film: demolished cathedrals spring up from the rubble; the grand embankments of the new canal system crumble into the muddy banks of the river Moscow. The Soviet ideal is destroyed. The audience is hysterical with laughter, and Alesha is frantic.

Finally, the situation is saved, and the film put in correctly. In a speech that recalls Zinka's tearless weeping in *The Miracle Worker*, implicitly directed at Comrade Stalin himself, Zoia introduces the film as it should be. She proclaims:

> Fulfilling the Stalin Plan for the Reconstruction of Moscow, the Moscow Bolsheviks have carried out a colossal task, our beloved Moscow has been transformed into the most magnificent capital. Great Stalin made this plan for reconstruction happen [...] Look what we have done to the town in the last three years alone!

As she speaks, the image of old Moscow, wooden and haphazard, is transformed. Gorky Street is widened, houses moved, bridges built, new canals filled with water. This, Zoia proclaims, is the Moscow of today.

Then follows the film's most grandiose moment – a vision of the capital *as it will be*. The present is blurred with the future, and the great work of construction becomes history in the making: new residential areas will spring up, connected by an ever-expanding metro; new rail routes will cross the city and territory; and the city will acquire a 'fairy tale beauty'. Finally, we see the new Palace of the Soviets, to be the tallest building in the world, rising from a newly constructed series of grand avenues and public squares (Figure 20). Topped by a gigantic statue of Lenin, it looms into the sky as planes fly in formation overhead.[11]

These scenes are the most complex and ambivalent in the film – and its ideological fulcrum. The son of Nina Alisova, the actress who played Zoia, speculates that this scene was the source of the film's banning. The old city that springs up out of the ruins of the new was, he suggests, too attractive; 'it becomes clear that Old Moscow, classical Moscow, [...] is so beautiful that none of it should be destroyed' – and this at the time of massive reconstruc-

19. Disaster: Alesha's film runs the wrong way (*New Moscow*, 1938)

tion.[12] Perhaps even more problematically, the scene is one of high comedy – not just for the spectator of the film, but for the on-screen audience at Alesha's presentation. Thus Medvedkin seems to make light of this most serious of projects.

Perhaps Medvedkin thought that the comically shocking destruction of the urban ideal would be fully compensated for by the grandeur of its reconstruction. As Chris Marker asks in the voice-over to his magisterial film on Medvedkin, 'Did you think that 10% conformity at the end would excuse the remaining 90%?' The situation is more complex than even Marker suggests, however, for it is not clear that the 'ideal' projection of the future city is itself unambiguously celebratory. With Medvedkin's characteristic taste for excess, this sequence is unique among representations of the Soviet capital – an apotheosis of the kind of idealised fantasies of the city that proliferated during the late 1930s and early 1940s. Medvedkin worked with the same cameraman, Igor Gelein, who had produced the much-praised 'poetic' landscapes of *The Miracle Worker*, and a similar hyperbolic 'realism' can be traced in these images. From a technical perspective, the sequence is a remarkable achievement. Using a blend of location filming and studio work, it manages to appear at once real and unreal – a combination that captures the genuinely fantastic nature of contemporary reconstruction projects.

20. The Palace of the Soviets, in the glorious future capital (*New Moscow*, 1938)

The city that Medvedkin pictures is, in very real terms, a dream city. In the grand plans for the construction of the Palace of the Soviets, to be the largest building in the world, of Moscow's magnificent canal network, etc., the General Plan was paper architecture, a vision as yet unrealised. In the geometrical patterns of his filmscape, Medvedkin captures the flavour of this paper architecture, of a city that existed in projects and aspirations but not in reality.

Down to Earth

Assessing the status of Medvedkin's vision of the ideal city is crucial to any understanding of the film. Oksana Bulgakova views the Moscow sequence as straightforwardly Utopian. Alesha, she suggests, is able to see Moscow more clearly from afar, and the model pictures what might be called the 'ideological city'– in Bulgakova's words, 'dematerialised architecture, the metaphysical space of visions and dreams'.[13] For the Soviet critic Iurenev, however, the Moscow sequence was the film's greatest weakness; lacking human life, it appeared as a 'dead' city.[14] Margolit and Shmyrov attribute the banning of the film to precisely this quality: the future Utopia appeared soulless and inhuman.[15]

This lifelessness was surely no accident: Medvedkin's Utopian city is characteristically ambivalent – it is majestic, certainly, but it is also *uninhabited*. And as such it contrasts with the energy and dynamism of the city in which his protagonists move. In his review of the film in January 1939, Ryklin noticed this. He praised the film's 'magnificent' shots of Moscow ('The cameraman should be congratulated,' he said), but claimed that they were poorly integrated into the film's comic plot. For him, these scenes were 'documentary', and bore little relation to the comic plot.

Ryklin's observation is pertinent. In fact, the disjuncture between the film's Utopian cityscape and its comic narrative is an essential part of Medvedkin's ironic comment on the Utopian ambitions of the Moscow plan. When the disgruntled Fedia, complaining about his constantly shifting vista, exclaims: 'Who is responsible for the landscape?' his words consciously exploit the dual meaning of the term 'landscape' (*peizazh* – at once a genre of painting, and the 'real' landscape of the city). They provide an ironic reflection on the Soviet ambition to make space political, to construct real space as image, to impose ideological visions on the physical world.

The irony of the film is most evident in its pointed 'normality'. We have seen how the carnival is a sanitised version of Medvedkin's popular buffonade. For all its fantastical images, *New Moscow* lacks the element of magic and enchantment that marked all Medvedkin's previous feature films, and most of his early work. Alesha's 'living model' enables a kind of virtual time travel, transporting its viewers from the past, through the present and into the future.

It does so, however (in his grandmother's words), 'not with miracles, but with technology!' – through the relatively prosaic device of a filmed mechanical model. Thus Medvedkin rejects the fantastic while dealing with one of the most fantastical of Soviet projects – the transformation of the capital. By contrast, in Alexandrov's *The Radiant Path* the heroine's celebratory journey to Moscow is carried out via the magical device of a flying automobile, and involves not only geographical displacement but time travel – Tania drives herself into her future. Thus Alexandrov represented the 'fairy tale' of Soviet achievement, in which the glorious future was just around the corner.

What Medvedkin provides, then, is a tongue-in-cheek representation of miracles brought down to earth. The moving houses that initially shock Alesha's grandmother and her sister are, in the end, normalised; the two women rescue house plants from the window sill and proceed with conversation. The literal uprooting of a home does little to disrupt everyday life; domestic space is little affected by the vagaries of public space. There is a greater significance here: in the end, the truth of the film is located in the interstices of the city in flux, in the domestic and lived spaces that remain somehow outside monumental change. And, in the context of the late 1930s, that message was deeply subversive.

Simulacra

In Alexandrov's *The Radiant Path* Tania's journey through space and time takes her not to the traditional centre of Moscow but to the site of the All-Union Exhibition, in its northern outskirts. This, then, represents the symbolic centre of the Soviet space. Medvedkin too gives the exhibition a central place in his film, and it provides an alternative perspective on the city, forming part of Medvedkin's playful enquiry into the nature of the city as both reality and symbol. All four of his young protagonists are involved in the exhibition. Zoia works there as a guide, and Alesha's model is brought to Moscow under its auspices; Fedia finds work producing advertising posters, and Olia brings her prize piglet to the show.

So, the exhibition unites our protagonists. It fulfils its historically sanctioned role: exhibiting the achievements 'of the people' to the people, the real All-Union Exhibition (first given a permanent home in Moscow in the same year that *New Moscow* was completed) was, from its very beginnings, presented in Soviet rhetoric as shared, a symbol of the involvement of *all* the peoples of the Soviet Union in the great process of transformation. In real terms, the developing architecture of the exhibition sites during the 1940s and 1950s created a space that functioned as a conceptual map of the Soviet territory: the diverse territories and peoples of the vast Soviet Union were represented, each with their own neoclassical pavilion decorated with images and shapes representative of regional specificity (wheat sheaves to symbolise the Ukraine as the 'breadbasket' of the Soviet Union, for example). As citizens of the ('single, multinational') Soviet Union, they were, implicitly, the same in essence, different only in detail.

In symbolic terms, film played its part in representing the exhibition as a site of symbolic unification, a simulacrum of the whole space of the nation. Like Medvedkin, Pyrev, in *The Swineherd and the Shepherd* [Svinarka i paskukh, 1941], used the exhibition as a meeting place, the site of a love story between two loyal citizens from opposite ends of the Soviet territory.[16] Moscow is the central and unifying space of the space, a romantic nexus. The exhibition was at once a real space and a symbol. And, as such, for Medvedkin it provides a microcosm of Moscow itself. Just as *The Miracle Worker*, with its exaggerated discourse on heroism, can be viewed as a parody of the production rhetoric of the time, so *New Moscow* parodies the cultural symbolisation of the city. Through its multiple spaces – the centre of the city, the exhibition, the carnival – it offers a composite vision of Moscow as simultaneously lived and imagined. The 'ideal' city is revealed as paper architecture, as pure fantasy; the 'real' city is chaotic, non-ideological and, above all, ordinary.

Transformation

The thematic centre of *New Moscow* is the idea of 'transformation', which extends to many of the film's disparate plots and parts. The city itself is transformed, both literally (in the moving of buildings) and symbolically (in Alesha's model). At Alesha's construction site, marshland is transformed into habitable space. In parallel, characters too undergo levels of transformation. During the masquerade they shift and mutate, assuming different guises and false identities. Within the film, they each undergo a process of self-transformation.

In the 'working version' of the screenplay, Medvedkin developed a subplot that lost emphasis in the final version of the film but that provides us with some insight into his preoccupations, and suggests some continuity between *New Moscow* and *The Miracle Worker*. At the beginning of the film Fedia is working on a picture, which we do not see, and for which Zoia is his model – his 'Gioconda', as he calls her, recalling Leonardo's *Mona Lisa*. The theme of the painting, as he describes it, is 'maternity'. After falling in love with Alesha, Zoia is no longer willing to pose for Fedia, and his painting is left unfinished, a symbol of his romantic tragedy. Later in the film, however, Fedia and the swineherd Olia fall happily in love themselves, and Fedia's romantic epiphany is expressed in his determination to paint Olia as 'a second Gioconda'– a 'happy mother'.

In the finished film, this sub-plot ends there. In the earlier screenplay, however, Fedia goes on to complete his painting on motherhood. Eventually he uses both women as his model mothers, and one of the film's final and triumphant scenes describes people reading about the painting in a newspaper, as 'Fedia conveys the theme of happy Soviet motherhood'.

This peculiar narrative may be seen as part of the ongoing play with categories of femininity that we identified in analysis of *The Miracle Worker*. Zoia and Olia represent different types of womanhood. Where Zoia is the coquettish urban beauty of a romantic comedy, whose natural environment is the department store and for whom leaving the capital is an almost unthinkable prospect, Olia is the sturdy, straightforward belle of rural life. Zoia, adored by two men, is not averse to playing one against the other, submitting Alesha to tests to prove his love. Capricious and demanding, she is, despite her Soviet pedigree, in many ways an archetypal romantic heroine of an earlier (and non-Soviet) time. Persuading Alesha to stay in Moscow, moreover, she attempts to lure him with the bourgeois entrapments of domestic space – an apartment in the centre, with gas, where she will bake pies for him.

Olia, by contrast, lacks such archetypal feminine wiles. Physically, too, she encapsulates a new ideal of femininity. Where Zoia, with her brunette prettiness, resembles the heroines of such earlier comedies as Room's *Bed and Sofa* or Barnet's *Girl with a Hatbox*, Olia has the sturdy, blond attractiveness of female stars such as Marina Ladynina (wife and chief actress of Pyrev in comedies such as *The Rich Bride*), often viewed as an archetype of the new Soviet beauty. Olia is in many ways a comic character, and the romance between her and Fedia is a comic foil to the more serious romance of the main protagonists.

Yet their story has a serious side: it is perhaps no accident that Olia represents Fedia's 'happy' Soviet mother. Fedia – trapped in the implicitly bourgeois ideals of old-fashioned 'art'– is rescued by Alesha and Olia. Through the former, and his magnificent model of Moscow, he discovers technology, and vows henceforward to 'build'. Through the latter, he discovers an implicitly healthy, constructive love. When the two meet for the first time at that lido on the banks of the river Moscow, he is overcome by sorrow at his failed love for Zoia. Olia's comment is emblematic: 'I always chase away sorrow with a smile … you know, I really advise you to try this method.' 'Thank you,' replies Fedia with despair; 'I envy your courage [*muzhestvo*].' The choice of word here, *muzhestvo*, is surely not accidental: from the masculine root, *muzh*, it endows Olia with a masculine fortitude that Fedia lacks. In her own way, Olia, a swineherd, is as practically involved in the Soviet project as Alesha. Becoming her lover, therefore, Fedia implicitly moves into a positive future. In a sense, he is a lesser version of Medvedkin's original 'idler', Khmyr;

his change provides a microcosmic version of the classic Socialist Realist story of 're-education'.

At another level, the transformation of Fedia can be read as a comment on the ideals of art. At the beginning of the film he is an archetypal 'artist'. His 'landscape' is that of the city, and it is in constant flux. For him, this is a transgression of an artist's basic role – his right to an undisturbed landscape or *natura* (nature, or model). At the beginning of the film, Fedia is positioned as onlooker and not participant; we meet him on a balcony, overlooking the city, hiding under a vast open parasol whenever things get difficult. He is, in the term familiar from nineteenth-century literature and reworked into the ideology of the Soviet period, 'superfluous' (*lishnii*). Ensconced within the symbolic armature of the romantic artist, surrounded by precisely the kind of vocabulary and ideals that Medvedkin was determined to reject, Fedia is afflicted by 'grief' when things do not go his way. He has no place in society – arguing with bureaucrats, unlucky in love. In his own words, he is a 'failure', who has no place in the world. Through his contact with Alesha and Olia, however, Fedia becomes a participant rather than an onlooker. First, he enlists his 'art' to celebrate the transformation of the city, rather than fighting against it. Second, in his love for Olia, and his painting of her, he enters the contemporary symbolic sphere – that of productive Sovietness.

Reception: A Parody of the Moscow Plan?

From an ideological perspective, then, this film is difficult to read. At a superficial level, it presents a glorification of the Soviet project. Through the dual transformation of the city and its protagonists, *New Moscow* seems to offer an unambiguous homage to the might and right of Stalin's Russia. As Fedia's art is enlisted in service of the state, he fulfils Medvedkin's often stated ideal. This positive reading of the film was put forward by Klado, in his pre-production assessment of the screenplay. Medvedkin's satire in *New Moscow*, Klado suggested, 'aimed at affirming the new and ridiculing the old'.[17] The film, moreover, was a further step on the director's 'path to realism'. Accordingly, *New Moscow* made it through the initial stages of censorship, and was completed and premiered to restricted audiences in January 1939. At the final stage, however, it was caught in the crossfire of this difficult time, and withdrawn from distribution. In a sense, Medvedkin was lucky; in the year that this film was shelved, Meyerhold and Babel were arrested. Meyerhold was executed in 1940. The world of culture was increasingly fraught with risk.

January 1939 was an inauspicious moment at which to release a new comedy. The previous year had been another difficult one for the Soviet cinematographic administration, and those who were ruled by it. In simple terms, not very many films were being made; in a climate of 'general plans' and Stakhanovite labour, film production was failing to live up to its own targets. Few screenplays passed the rigours of censorship and political intervention. Others, like *The Accursed Force*, were stopped further down the production line. In January 1938 an essay in the Party newspaper *Pravda* complained of a film 'famine', and laid the blame on Shumiatsky (by this time Deputy Chairman of the Committee for Artistic Affairs).[18] A few days later, he was arrested as a 'Trotskyite'. In March 1938, after an administrative reshuffle, Semen Dukelsky was appointed head of the new Committee of Cinematography (under the Council of Commissars, directly affiliated to central administration). This appointment did not signal a relaxation of censorship, however. Quite the opposite: Dukelsky's job was to 'reorganise', to bring order to the unruly world of Soviet cinematography.[19]

It is tempting to speculate on the reasons why *New Moscow* was 'shelved', but there is little to go on. A review of the film appeared in *Pravda* in January (the first time that one of Medvedkin's feature films had been considered in that most official of newspapers), and gave no hint of the fate that was to befall the film.[20] The reviewer praised Medvedkin's ongoing investment in the troublesome comic genre, but accused him of 'carelessness'. *New Moscow* had 'comic incidents', but lacked the essential 'lyricism' of good Soviet comedy: 'The spectator looks for warm, sincere feeling in its positive heroes,' Ryklin wrote, and *New Moscow* did not provide them.[21] It was dramatically 'weak' and poorly structured.

In practice, the 'ideal' Soviet comedy remained more dream than reality: of the seventeen feature films produced and distributed by the central studios during 1938, only one (Alexandrov's *Volga Volga*) was classified as a 'comedy'. Meanwhile, other, less troublesome, genres dominated the Soviet screen. After the problems of *Bezhin Meadow*, Eisenstein's historical epic *Alexander Nevsky* premiered in 1938, to significant acclaim. The first part of another historical epic, Vladimir Petrov's *Peter I*, also appeared. At the same time the third and final part of Kozintsev and Trauberg's *Maxim* trilogy, *The Vyborg Side* [Vyborgskaia storona, 1938], was completed, acclaimed as a signal achievement in Socialist Realist cinema. The *Maxim* trilogy followed the gradual transformation of an unruly young man, Maxim, into a hero of the Revolution. It was, in a sense, a fictionalised biography of the Soviet nation itself, represented in the biography of a single hero, at once ordinary and exceptional. This genre of Revolutionary drama was increasingly dominant in the second half of the 1930s.

According to Ryklin, then, *New Moscow* was simply 'unsuccessful', a comedy that failed to find a place within the ideological paradigms of Soviet film-making in the late 1930s. In his work on Medvedkin, Iurenev concurred with this assessment of the film's weakness, but claimed to see 'no reason' for its banning.[22] Others have laid the blame squarely on the striking image of the socialist Utopia collapsing, the transformation of the centre into periphery, the capital into provincial town – the visual destruction of progress.

Certainly, Medvedkin seems to take a playful swipe at the same Utopian fantasies that the film ostensibly glorifies. I would suggest that his subversion of cultural mythology extends much further into the film, however. In the end, this is a film about chaos, about the metropolitan adventures of young lovers in a city that is changing around them. It offers a dual image of the capital as reality and symbol, as lived space and fantasy space. Ultimately, in contrast to the energy of the real city, the fantasy space appears simply absurd. And it was surely this that made the film seem such a political risk.

7. Journeys in the Lands of Evil

Despite the suppression of *New Moscow*, Medvedkin's commitment to cinema seems to have been undented. He remained a prominent figure in the Soviet film community, and did not entirely abandon his comic ambitions. In August 1939 he made a speech about the importance of comedy at a meeting of film directors and administrators (including Pyrev, Alexander Dovzhenko, Mikhail Romm and the new head of the Committee for Cinematography, Bolshakov), devoted to the 'problem' of film narrative.[1] Between 1939 and 1940 he prepared a second version of *The Accursed Force* and submitted it to Mosfilm under an alternative title, *The Blessed Lot* [Svetlaia dolia].[2] In practice, however, the fate of *New Moscow* represented an end point. Later in 1939 Medvedkin was asked to head a team of film-makers to record a 'physical culture' parade on Red Square.[3] This seems to have been intended as a kind of palliative, and it marked a decisive move into documentary film-making for Medvedkin – the end of his first dream of political satire.

The Film Soldier

After the collapse of the Nazi-Soviet pact in 1941, however, when the Soviet Union went to war, there were more important things for this former soldier and committed activist to think about. Medvedkin's first involvement with what Stalin proclaimed as the 'Great Patriotic War' was straightforward propaganda: he produced a short musical 'film-concert' entitled *We Await Your Victorious Return* [My zhdem vas s pobedoi], which came out in July 1941. This film – the first of what became a popular genre of wartime 'film-concerts' – consisted of eight musical 'numbers', strung together by a loose plot. It showed soldiers leaving their village for the front; in their absence, the desolate but resolute young women of the village assume responsibility for the business of the farm.

In its synchronised dance and song routines, *We Await Your Victorious Return* resembles the Hollywood musical *Seven Brides for Seven Brothers* [1954], but lacks any developed narrative. With its overtly idealised representation of a Russian 'folk' spirit, it is a hymn to the strengths of the nation facing war. Its ritualised and joyful folk entertainment is brought to a pointedly brutal end as the boys finally head to battle, and real documentary footage of war explodes into the pastoral idyll, leaving the spectator shattered by the coming trial. Meanwhile, the real battle was beginning, and in the autumn of 1941, faced with the rapid advance of the enemy towards Moscow, all film studios were evacuated out of the capital, and Alma-Ata in Kazakhstan became the head-quarters of a merged Mosfilm and Lenfilm. In November Medvedkin himself was posted to Baku, in Azerbaijan.[4]

Although the production of feature films to support the war effort was important, the more important task was played by documentary film. Soviet film-makers were soon busy at the front – shooting, according to Peter Kenez, approximately three and a half million metres of film over the course of the war.[5] In 1942 a new Central Studio for Documentary Film was established in Moscow, the command centre for an increasingly organised system of war reporting.[6] Teams of film-makers at the front sent footage back to the central base to be edited, and newsreels appeared in cinemas in major cities every three days.

Reared in the State Military Film Organisation, Medvedkin the soldier had long prepared for direct action, and, as always, film was to be his weapon.[7] Trapped and frustrated in Baku, he was full of ideas: in February 1942 he presented a detailed proposal to Bolshakov for mobile film 'depots' in trucks, which would do for the war what the film-train had done for the Five-Year Plan, increasing 'the political role of documentary film in the mobilisation of forces against the threat of fascism'.[8]

Although this particular project came to nothing, Medvedkin did eventually become involved in an innovative cinematographic experiment. In late 1943 he was transferred to become head of a team of film-makers on the 'Third Belorussian Front' near Minsk, sending footage back to the Central Studio. He worked well; the archive contains a report of an official meeting of the administrative committee of the Documentary film studio, when Medvedkin's team were congratulated on the quality and value of their work.[9] Buoyed by this success, he wrote to its head, Sergei Gerasimov, in September 1944, asking for desperately needed extra manpower.[10] That support was not forthcoming, however, and Medvedkin had a characteristically Revolutionary idea: to equip ordinary soldiers with sixteen-millimetre film cameras. This would solve the problem of manpower, and do much more besides; it would provide unique 'real-life' material from the front. No film-maker, after all, could be as close to action as a soldier.

In March 1945 the first 'soldiers with cameras' began to work on the front, and their footage formed part of a film, *In the Wolf's Lair (Eastern Prussia)* [V logove zveria (Vostochnaia Prussiia)] produced late that month. The experiment was a success and for once Medvedkin's timing was good; as the Soviet army moved towards victory, Medvedkin gained unique and well-timed access to the 'real' heroism of the front line, and his reports were invariably able to celebrate its latest triumphs.[11] By May the war was over, and the work of the 'soldiers with cameras' came to a premature end; 'I will always regret that we were so late in giving film cameras to soldiers,' Medvedkin wrote later.[12]

The Liberated Land

After the Allied victory Medvedkin moved to Sverdlovsk (now Ekaterinburg), where he produced a feature film, *The Liberated Land* [Osvobozhdennaia zemlia]. Here, for the first time, he worked with a screenplay that was not his own, called in to save the day on a script that had been accepted for production but considered unsuccessful.[13] Working at his characteristic pace, he completed production of the film by July of the same year.

The finished film tells the story of a community returning to their village after German occupation. As it opens, we see a lone cart crossing a desolate landscape, heading 'home', only to find their village destroyed, burned almost to the ground by the marauding enemy. Undeterred, the resilient heroine of the film, Nadezhda, becomes the de facto leader of the group, working to rebuild their ruined home. Kind and welcoming (her name means 'hope'), Nadezhda takes in a decommissioned soldier and agricultural expert, Foma, who has lost his wife and children. While they rebuild their homes the group take up residence in the old school, and Nadezhda persuades the benign local authorities to provide them with help. With a tragic twist, just as life begins to improve she receives the shattering news of the death of her husband, and her children. The rest of the film tracks the rebirth of the village and of Nadezhda in parallel. Towards the end of the film, the community's dreams come true; through negotiation with the head of the local machine tractor station (MTS: these were rural depots that would hire out machinery), played by Alexander Medvedkin himself, they acquire that most valuable of Soviet commodities – a tractor. When the children of the decommissioned officer are miraculously found unharmed Nadezha becomes their surrogate mother, and, through her love for them and – eventually – for their father, she rediscovers joy.

The film is a curious hybrid of melodrama and playfulness. One of its most successful elements is the figure of old Grandfather Murliuk. This character, with his repeated exclamation 'Grief of griefs' and penchant for vodka, is classically Medvedkin-esque, playfully and appealingly comic, while at the same time serving as a voice of common sense and emotional support for all members of the community. His daughter, the coquettish young Daria, for whom hard work is something of a trial, does not escape Medvedkin's satirical eye; she is endearingly flighty but nonetheless subject to significant ridicule, with the implicit message that, with her bourgeois ways, she hinders the progress of socialism.

These comic elements sit somewhat strangely within the heightened sentimentality of the narrative, and against the tragic fortitude of Nadezhda (played by Emma Tsesarskaia, statuesque heroine of Alexander Strizhak's *Her Way* [Ee put', 1929] and Konstantin Iudin's *A Girl with Character* [Devushka s kharakterom, 1939]). A similar heterogeneity – even discord – is evident at the level of style. In places, Medvedkin adopts the stylised immobility of landscape art. As the villagers learn of the destruction of their village, for example, they are pictured frozen in anguish against the contours of the ravaged landscape. After Nadezhda receives news of her terrible tragedy we see her alone in the fields, and a mournful soundtrack creates an image of woman and nature united in grief – in grief, implicitly, for all those lost in war. In other sequences, by contrast, the landscape is straightforwardly lyrical and full of hope, firmly positioned within the timelessness of the pastoral tradition, as the villagers scythe the fields. Elsewhere we see traces of Medvedkin's former Chaplinesque antics, as Grandfather Murliuk gets drunk and falls down, to be rescued by a laughingly tolerant Nadezhda.

For once, Medvedkin did not succeed in making this curious mixture work, and the film was not well reviewed. Distressed, he wrote directly to Andrei Zhdanov, the powerful Party chief for cultural affairs in July 1946, claiming that the criticisms were unfounded.[14] Two weeks later he seems to have regretted the rashness of that action; in a letter to a lesser bureaucrat he expressed remorse, asking him to ensure that Zhdanov did not misunderstand his intentions.[15]

Emergency Service

Such circumspection was wise, for these were dangerous years for Soviet film-makers. Cinema was more closely affiliated to the state than ever before: Bolshakov was made Minister of Cinema in 1946, and the semi-independent Committee for Cinema Affairs was dissolved. The signs were ominous; on 4 September 1946 the Party's Central Committee issued a threatening resolution criticising two films (Part Two of Leonid Lukov's *A Great Life* [Bol'shaia zhizn', 1946] and Eisenstein's *Ivan the Terrible* [Ivan Groznyi, 1946]). 'Workers in the arts should understand that those who continue to act irresponsibly and thoughtlessly in connection with their work will easily find themselves outside of the most advanced Soviet art and fall away.'[16]

In addition to such ideological pitfalls, film-makers faced a new economic situation. The Ministry of Cinema announced that the number of films produced would be limited. In 1948 only seventeen feature films were made, and by 1951 that number had been reduced to a mere nine films. This period, known retrospectively as the years of 'film hunger' (*malokartin'e*), was the darkest that the beleaguered film industry had yet endured. The path from scenario to film became even more perilous than it had been in the 1930s. Censorship seems to have operated more or less arbitrarily, as lower-level officials struggled to anticipate the changing Party line.

It was in this difficult environment that Medvedkin produced his next feature, and experimented with a new medium: animation. Although he had worked extensively with animation on the film-train, *Emergency Service* [Skoraia pomoshch', 1949] was Medvedkin's first complete cartoon, produced to his screenplay by the animator Lamis Bredis. This was the beginning and the end of Medvedkin's brief flirtation with fully animated cinema; it was banned before its release in 1949.[17]

On the surface, *Emergency Service* seems to have an ideal plot for these years of political retrenchment. It features a sinister capitalist snake, the millionaire Mr Boa (Mister Udav), dressed in a fur coat and driving around in a sports car bearing the sign 'Emergency Services'. In a thinly veiled allegory of capitalism, Mr Boa has devised a complex plot to exploit rabbits – promising American cigarettes and leather jackets in return for their furs. He persuades an innocent young male rabbit, Totti, to relinquish his scraggy pelt in exchange for a rather natty leather blouson. Totti agrees, hoping that his new look will secure him the love of the attractive young bunny, Mummi.

Thus converted, Totti works for Mr Boa in persuading his comrade bunnies to relinquish their fur. Thus he becomes inadvertently complicit in their exploitation; once stripped, the rabbits are swindled and left shivering in the cold, and the promised leather jackets are not provided. All is not lost, however. The innocent masses are eventually saved by wise and cynical hedgehogs (explicitly represented as Bolshevik intellectuals), who see through the capitalist's evil scheme and encourage the rabbits to revolt. As the film ends, they burn the corrupt Western goods that have been used to bribe them, and retreat to their burrows to plan their revolution.

Emergency Service, then, represents another failed attempt at political satire. It is a clear attempt to engage with the political and social realities of the

Soviet Union in the difficult post-war years.[18] The film is a warning to Soviet citizens, now increasingly aware – through their military advance into Western Europe, time spent in prisoner-of-war camps abroad, and collaboration with the Allies – of the gulf in living standards between the Soviet Union and the West. It is a warning not to be lured by Western promises, however difficult life might be: the workers' Revolution, symbolised by the hedgehogs' mass meeting at the end of the film, will eventually prove victorious.

Medvedkin trod too close to the line, however. In a report on the film, signed by Bolshakov, it was described as 'fallacious' (*porochnym*) and accused of ideological errors.[19] The authors were accused of 'vulgarising' the important political theme of reactionary imperialist politics, and the film was banned. The results, moreover, were far-reaching: Bredis, the film's director, was never allowed to direct again; other members of the studio were punished for having allowed it to be produced at all; and Medvedkin was forbidden from any further work with the animation studio.

A Tireless Spring

In this difficult climate, then, it is scarcely surprising that Medvedkin retreated from the dangerous field of comedy. During the early 1950s he produced a number of newsreels for the daily news programme, *News of the Day* [Novosti dnia] – an occupation scarcely fitting for a director of Medvedkin's now considerable experience and standing. Survival was at stake, however; the pointed satire that had caused him so many problems in the 1930s was unlikely to find a sympathetic audience. By a strategy of avoidance, Medvedkin managed to negotiate the demands of the period with relative success, maintaining his status within the artistic elite.

After the death of Stalin in 1953 things began to change. In the struggle for succession it was eventually Nikita Khrushchev who held sway, and the period now known as the 'Thaw' began. The gradual dismantling of the Stalin cult began shortly after his death, and gathered pace with Nikita Khrushchev's famous speech at the 20th Party Congress in 1956. This 'secret speech', which rapidly became known all over Russia, sanctioned a new political openness, the relaxing of cultural restrictions. A new generation of Soviet film-makers, and a new direction in film-making, took their first tentative steps.

The effects of the Thaw on Soviet cinema were profound – more immediately far-reaching, perhaps, than in any other cultural medium. As Alexander Prokhurov describes it, 'anti-monumentalism and a yearning for self-expression capable of restoring the Revolutionary spirit lost under Stalin became the new values of the era'.[20] In the work of a new, younger generation of film-makers, the ideological clarity of late Stalinism began to break down. In 1956 Grigori

Chukhrai's groundbreaking film *The Forty-First* [Sorok pervyi] told a story of the Civil War in which a young female soldier in the Red Army falls in love with her prisoner, a member of the White Guard. The film, in which human relationships stand outside – and challenge – ideological certainties, signalled the beginning of this new wave, and the film won a special prize at Cannes in 1957. In the same year two other young directors, Marlen Khutsiev and Felix Miromer, produced *Spring on Zarechnaia Street* [Vesna na Zarechnoi ulitse, 1956], another film about love, in which the collective is virtually absent and the young protagonist is shown to be sensitive and vulnerable – not to social forces, but to the emotional challenges of his lover. In this film, as in many others of the period, landscape – ever a symbol of the grandeur of Soviet power – was conscripted as a metaphor, a means of representing what Evgeni Margolit calls 'the journey of the human soul'.[21]

As always, Medvedkin – member of the original Revolutionary generation and self-styled 'propaganda officer' – remained closer to politics than to 'art'. In February 1954 Khrushchev launched a campaign for the transformation of the 'virgin lands', with the ambitious intention of using massive irrigation projects to turn the barren and inhospitable spaces of the vast Soviet Union (Kazakhstan, Siberia and the Urals) into fertile agricultural plains. Medvedkin the agitator, ever at the forefront of such initiatives, was in the Kazakh Republic between 1954 and 1958, filming the successes and trials of the 'Virgin Lands' campaign.[22] In addition to 'safe' propaganda work, he must have felt that, in this more relaxed political climate, the conditions were right for him to try his hand at comedy again, and he produced a feature entitled *A Spring without Rest* [Bespokoinara vesna, 1956].

This comedy about the 'Virgin Lands' projects was a classically Socialist Realist narrative of an individual's 're-education': this time, the hapless 'idler' was a leather-jacket-clad young musician called Zhenia. Arriving with a band of enthusiastic young Komsomol members to build a new town in the steppe, Zhenia initially lacks the energy and commitment that characterises the rest of the group. Although his dream, like that of all the young participants, is 'to become a tractor driver and a hero', he isn't prepared to work for the honour.

Zhenia is a modern-day version of Medvedkin's original 'idler', Khmyr. Indeed, the parallels are explicit: just as Khmyr's initial job on his collective farm was to drive the water cart that serviced the tractors that ploughed the field, so it is a sign of Zhenia's failure as a worker that he too begins his work as a water carrier. Like Khmyr, he begins as an idler; at the beginning of the film he falls asleep at his work. Unsuccessful even in love, he falls for a young beauty, but she prefers the muscular young Kazakh tractor driver Idris.

Eventually, of course, Zhenia does exhibit the necessary initiative and determination, and ascends to the valued profession of tractor driver. Thus

Medvedkin offered an ideologically appropriate narrative of transformation. The strength of the film, however, lies not in its central narrative but in the side plots and characters, which show traces of Medvedkin's former mocking eye. The local bureaucrat responsible for supplying the Komsomol with vital provisions, for example, is delightfully inept: on one occasion he arrives with hundreds of pairs of galoshes instead of much-needed food for the workers. Another character is an ideological 'enthusiast', always with a newspaper in his pocket and an idea in his head (recalling the inimitable Savva, with his head so buried in the news of the nation that he ignores his donkey's digressions), but unable to match the simple energy and down-to-earth commitment of the others. Zhenia, too, is treated to Medvedkin's comic touch: just as Khmyr was memorably attached to his voracious dappled horse, so Zhenia forms a peculiar relationship with the horse that pulls his water cart, which is shown at one point laughing at his master's ineptitudes.

A Spring without Rest is a curious film. For all its comic flourishes, it remains a limited narrative of social re-education. We have little emotional engagement with the characters, who remain broadly two-dimensional. Zhenia's transformation is, in the end, unconvincing in both social and personal terms. From an orthodox ideological perspective, it is unclear whether he is motivated by anything other than the desire to overcome his shame and to fit in. Yet nor is he given the psychological depth or personal appeal that would make the film interesting in human terms.

In a sense, this is a transitional film – indicative, perhaps, of Medvedkin's ambivalent relationship with the society that was beginning to change around him. It is caught between different eras of film-making, between changing imperatives. Focusing on Zhenia's path to political consciousness, it offers a standard Socialist Realist narrative. With its theme of land reclamation, moreover, it represents landscape not according to the emergent poetic trend but according to earlier Socialist Realist models: the submission of nature to the might of man. It opens with a striking technicolour panorama, showing a formidably empty steppe, marked only by a tiny, somewhat premature, sign announcing that this is the 'Collective Farm Mai-Balk'. Over the course of the film, a new town does indeed emerge out of the inhospitable landscape.

Yet, within this apparent conformity to a previous ideal, the film is nevertheless of its time. Zhenia, with his guitar and leather jacket, is a quintessential representative of a new generation. His aspirations are confused; he parrots the official doctrine of 'wishing to become a tractor driver', yet sleeps all day and dreams of love. As such, in him, we see the glimmering of a new and more complex understanding of the real nature of the Soviet 'hero'. It is this ambivalence at the heart of the film that is its downfall.

Cinematic Journeys

A Spring without Rest was Medvedkin's only realised feature film of the Thaw years. Back in Moscow in 1959 – having, in his own words, 'already reached pensionable age'[23] – he does not seem to have been greatly touched by the cinematic new wave. Not for him, soldier of the first Revolution, the self-examination of the younger generation. Indeed, the emphasis on individuality and subjectivity so evident in the new films of young directors seems to run directly counter to Medvedkin's deep-rooted belief in public cinema. The drive towards the representation of ordinariness, of the everyday stories of individual life that gently subverted the grand narratives of Socialist Realism, so emblematic of Soviet cinema of this period, did not sit easily with Medvedkin's love of the burlesque and exaggeration.

In contrast, moreover, to the anti-ideological stance adopted by many younger film-makers during the late 1950s and early 1960s, Medvedkin continued to believe in the value of cinema as educator.[24] Retreating from the feature film arena, he embarked, however, on a new and productive phase of his career, which he later described as his 'journey in the world of evildoers'.[25] Between 1959 and his death in 1989 Medvedkin made some eighteen documentary film 'essays' for the Central Studio of Documentary Film.

These films make interesting watching, providing a new perspective on Medvedkin as political animal, increasingly despairing of the world around him but always upholding his firm commitment to the regime he served. They document the political imperatives of the Cold War years, and the director's passionate engagement. In all these films he turns his critical eye abroad, and it seems, as Viktor Demin observed, as though 'alarm signals from all over the world have pierced the soul of the artist'.[26] In all of them he used the same method: the re-editing of pre-existent footage from diverse sources in order to create his own montage, given structure and meaning by a voice-over, usually provided by Medvedkin himself.[27] His angry narrative aimed, as he put it, to leave 'no place for a second opinion', and he brought the full weight of his substantial experience to bear.[28]

The first of the film 'pamphlets' was *Attention! Rockets on the Rhine!* [Vnimanie! Rakety na Reine!, 1959]. It examined the opposing political regimes of East and West Germany, with a resounding vote of support for the Communist East. Further afield, *The Law of Baseness* [Zakon podlosti, 1962] turned its attention to Africa, and to the impact of Western colonialism and racism. As usual, Medvedkin pulled few punches: earlier plans for a film about Africa had included plans for animated sequences with a 'bear businessman' and a 'wolf with a conscience'.[29] In an extensive montage, the film included footage of racism in the West, of living standards in African states, and of

United Nations meetings, all drawn together to present a theory of a repressive Western conspiracy of which Africa was the victim. In 1966, after the official break in trade relations between the Soviet Union and Mao Zedong's People's Republic of China, and the suspension of aid to Communist China, Medvedkin began a series of films about the Chinese 'problem'.

The Evil West

The principal enemy, however, was the capitalist and imperialist West. 'It is difficult to enumerate the evildoers who replace one another at the helm of the capitalist world,' Medvedkin wrote.[30] His attack began in earnest in 1960 as the nuclear threat began to increase. *Reason against Madness* [Razum protiv bezumiia 1960] was the first of a succession of films that operate squarely within the ideological discourse of the Cold War. In it, the Soviet Union is pictured as a democratic state; the West is accused of imperialist ambitions and, moreover, of broadly destructive intentions with regard to the world at large, through the development of chemical and nuclear weapons.

Meanwhile, things were changing at home. In 1964 the Central Committee voted to remove Khrushchev from office, to be replaced by Leonid Brezhnev. In 1966, at the 23rd Party Congress, the image of Stalin underwent a partial rehabilitation. In 1969 Alexander Solzhenitsyn was excluded from the Writers' Union after the publication abroad of his *Gulag Archipelago*. The signs were clear: the latter part of the 1960s and the subsequent decade, often described as the 'stagnation', saw a significant political and cultural retrenchment.

None of this seems to have altered Medvedkin's commitment to the pro-Soviet and anti-Western cause, however. On the contrary, closely in step with the rhetoric of the Cold War, he continued to produce his filmed attacks on the imperialist West. Indeed, in 1968, with *The Forgetful Conscience* [Sklevoz sovesti], he launched his most scathing attack so far. In a letter to Marker, Medvedkin described this film as 'a pamphlet, in which I try to recount the destruction of moral norms and the moral degradation of contemporary capitalist society'.[31] The director's voice-over opens the film with a portentous warning: 'The conscience of man! We observe with alarm how, year after year, in the West, this priceless capital is lost.' Shots of innocent children are cross-cut with the faces of Franco, Mussolini and other 'evildoers'. A list of so-called 'victims of terror' – including Martin Luther King alongside the brothers Robert and John F. Kennedy– is enumerated, and Christianity is shown to be morally corrupt.

In the 1970s, still with the West in view, Medvedkin turned his attention to nature. *A Chronicle of Alarm* [Trevozhnaia khronika, 1972] is an impassioned attack on the 'barbarous' destruction and pollution of the environment brought about by (capitalist) scientific 'advance'. Animal experimentation is attacked, ecological catastrophe – brought about by biological and nuclear weapons – is predicted, and the human risks of radiation and polluted water are spelt out. This film (made fourteen years before the disastrous human and ecological consequences of the explosion at the nuclear power station in Chernobyl in 1986) shows Medvedkin's ongoing concern about the growing nuclear threat, and it was in 1983, the year that Ronald Reagan described the Soviet Union as the 'evil empire' and launched his infamous 'Star Wars' campaign, that he began his final film. In *The Alarm* [Trevoga 1984], which carried the subtitle 'Thoughts of an old man', Medvedkin used his own age and experience as a device through which to offer a critique of the contemporary world, linking his own physical decline with what he saw as the decline of the world, and expressing worry about future generations: 'Do not ask of me respect, or diplomatic caution, with regard to these idiots who are ready to destroy our planet!'

In the mid-1980s, however, shortly after this film was completed, change began to be felt on the international stage. In 1985 Ronald Reagan and the new General Secretary, Mikhail Gorbachev, issued a historic joint statement on cooperation in nuclear arms reduction, signalling the beginning of the end of the Cold War – and of the Soviet Union. Medvedkin's anti-Westernism was not easily shaken. In 1985, in letters to Leyda, he asked 'a delicate question'; having finally signed a publication contract with Harvard University Press in 1983, he had one significant concern: would Harvard University Press back out of their contract with him 'if this, my last film, were to be an attack on the insane nuclear confrontation'?[32] In 1986 he wrote a letter to Mikhail Gorbachev himself, in which he defended and explained his anti-American stance – clearly anxious to ensure that he remained in step with official ideology.[33] As the world changed around him, Medvedkin held firm to his beliefs.

Real Journeys: The International Connections

Medvedkin's work during this period was part of what Margolit has described as a significant revival of documentary cinema in the Soviet Union in the mid-1960s.[34] In 1965 Mikhail Romm, whose workshop at the All-Union State Cinema Institute became the 'cradle' of the new generation of film-makers during the Thaw (among students enrolled were Andrei Tarkovsky, Larisa Shepitko, Gleb Panfilov and Vasili Shukshin), produced his own remarkable full-length feature/documentary, *Ordinary Fascism* [Obyknovennyi fashism], offering a damning indictment of the rise of fascist regimes in the West. Like Medvedkin's films, it consisted of a collage of edited footage, accompanied by a read monologue (written by the film scholar Maya Turovskaya).

This coincidence in technique indicates that Medvedkin was not entirely outside the key trends of film-making during the Thaw years. Although he was not a direct participant in the cinematic renaissance of the period moveover, he did feel its benefits. In the 1960s *Happiness* enjoyed something of a revival. It was shown in the first Moscow International Film Festival in 1959, as part of a retrospective of the masterpieces of Soviet cinema, and its renown rapidly spread to an international audience, sparking a new adventure for Medvedkin. Marker first saw *Happiness* in Brussels during a Soviet cinema retrospective. 'There was an unknown film, made by an unknown, a superb film, as good as Eisenstein, as popular as Mussorgsky music, astonishing: Alexander Medvedkin's *Happiness*,' he later recalled. 'Where was the director? Dead or alive?'[35] Medvedkin and Marker finally met at the International Festival of Documentary Film in Leipzig in 1967, and a remarkable friendship ensued – evidenced in the fascinating correspondence between the two film-makers, which continued more or less regularly from 1968 until Medvedkin's death.[36]

It was at their first meeting in Leipzig that Medvedkin told Marker about his film-train experiment. For the younger man, it was evidently a revelation – and a lesson that Marker was quick to convey to his radical colleagues back in France. Marker's left-wing film production 'cooperative' (a group that included Michel Derois, René Vautier and Hervet Pernot, and carried the name SLON [the acronym for Société pour le Lancement des Oeuvres Nouvelles, and also the Russian for 'elephant']) began to spread the word. Hearing of Medvedkin, a group of workers in a factory in Besançon, whose aim was to produce films about their own working conditions as a form of political protest, decided to call themselves 'the Medvedkin Group'.

The admiration of these French radicals for the septagenarian director seems to have known no bounds: in a letter to Medvedkin in January 1970 their leader, Paul Cèbe, wrote on headed paper with the title 'The Medvedkin Group, Besançon', and playfully signed himself 'Medvedkinement' (Medvedkinly – replacing the French 'cordially' [amicalement]).[37] In return, Medvedkin wrote several letters to the group, in which he recounted the lessons that he had learned on the train, emphasising the power and value of such locally orientated cinema. 'To see yourself, your friends, your street on screen is always a disconcerting event in the life of anyone. In our time we realised this quickly, and used it as the most powerful lever in the search for genres of active political cinema.'[38]

In January 1971 the seventy-one-year-old director spent a few days in Paris with Cèbe and Marker, during which the younger men showed Medvedkin the work of the Besançon group, and made filmed interviews with him at a railway depot on the outskirts of Paris as he told the story of his film-train. During this time, Cèbe recalled, 'Medvedkin talked and talked and talked'.

In an appealing anecdote, he recounts how they had arranged for Medvedkin to work with three interpreters per day, organised as shifts. In practice, however, these three turned out to be insufficient; Medvedkin would simply not stop talking, and Marker had to organise a fourth interpreter to cover the full twenty-four hour period…

Later that year Marker added a musical track to *Happiness* and organised a screening of the film in the Alpha Club in Paris in December, accompanied by his first short film about the director (which used the footage taken during Medvedkin's earlier trip to Paris), entitled *And the Train Rolls On…* [*Le train en marche*, 1971]. The screenings caused a sensation in the French press, and a flurry of interviews with Marker, reviews, etc. appeared.[39] All this press had a dual focus: it emphasised the power and novelty of *Happiness*, and discussed the innovation of the film-train. Marker was at pains to emphasise Medvedkin's remarkably early understanding of the power of cinema as a precursor to television. He emphasised the extraordinary technical capacity that had enabled film processing to take place while the train was in motion, pointing out that Medvedkin had spotted the vital power of visual media in the representation of the local and the immediate.

Medvedkin's growing international connections provided him with the opportunity to travel abroad. After his first trip to Paris he travelled to London in February 1971, staying at the King's Court Hotel near Hyde Park. 'This morning,' he wrote in his diary, 'I take my ferst brekfast [sic].'[40] These foreign trips had a professional justification: his task, here and in Paris, was to find evidence of the evils of capitalism to support his anti-Western films. He made notes on the 'growth and poverty' of the population, on 'children and pollution', on 'the destruction of the forests'. At the same time, however, he did find time to make a pilgrimage to 'a pub where Marx used to drink'.

Slowly, Medvedkin's feature films acquired an international reputation. In 1977 he travelled to Stockholm, where he was present at a screening of *Happiness* on 1 March, and then it was back to Paris for a screening of *The Miracle Worker*.[41] Meanwhile, the waves of his influence spread to Italy (Medvedkin had an extensive correspondence with the Marxist critic Guido Aristarco), to South America (his essay on the film-train, '294 Days on Wheels', was published in Buenos Aires in 1973), to Germany (Medvedkin had a correspondence with the film-maker Peter Krieg) and elsewhere.

All these relationships – especially that with Marker – were immeasurably important to Medvedkin. They offered him a level of recognition that he was never accorded in his own country. And, in the radical political extremism of the young Frenchmen, he found a reflection of his own deep-rooted belief in the power of film as a weapon in the battle for communism. While in Paris, in March 1977, he wrote in his diary that Marker was 'a friend like I've never had before'.[42] His letters to Marker are remarkable for their effusion and emotion: in his last letter, written in January 1989 when he was already very ill and 'broken down by old age,' he wrote, 'I embrace you and want to see you more often. OUR FRIENDSHIP MUST HAVE NO END.'[43] Thus, this anti-Western campaigner found his closest companionship in the West. During the difficult years of the Soviet 'stagnation'; this support from abroad convinced him of the necessity and value of his work, of the validity of his early beliefs; in a sense, it kept the old Bolshevik in Medvedkin alive.

Conclusions: The Other Story

All this, then, is the public story of Medvedkin's post-war career. But there is a parallel tale – one that sheds a different light on this most complex of characters. It is the private story – of the films the director did not make, of the many screenplays that he wrote, rewrote and abandoned over the course of his career. This story is, in many ways, a tragic one. It speaks of a frustrated imagination, of a commitment to a dream that was never realised.

There are around a hundred unrealised screenplays in Medvedkin's archive. They show the director trying to negotiate the changing political imperatives of his time, but also continuing along his own determinedly different path. The man who on the surface appeared to be a documentary film-maker was, in private, a comic author, but one whose most cherished works were destined never to see the light of day. In addition to the great, ongoing project of *The Accursed Force*, his private passion, Medvedkin's creative life was marked by a series of unfulfilled dreams. It is this duality at the heart of his career, and the curious blend of apparent political conformity with stylistic ambivalence, that make him such a fascinating, and complex, object of study.

With his uncanny awareness of the shifting paradigms of rhetoric, there can be no doubt that Medvedkin, of all people, was aware of what was happening to his Revolutionary ideal. As early as 1947 he wrote an unrealised screenplay that can be seen as a wry observation of how the Soviet dream had changed. The first part of *A Song about the Future*, a 'fantastic film', is entitled 'The Return of Mayakovsky', and is something of an homage to that Revolutionary poet.[44] Like Maiakovsky's own satirical play of 1929, *The Bedbug*, in which the grotesque Prisypkin is resurrected into an ostensibly Utopian future, so in this film Maiakovsky himself is reborn in the post-war Soviet Union. 'There was an unusual occurrence in the Tretiakov Gallery ...' the screenplay begins, as Maiakovsky's portrait comes slowly to life. Frustrated by the immobility of his pose as a painting, this 'tumultuous' poet breaks out of his frame, shouting a rewritten version of his famous poem, 'At the top of my voice' ['Vo ves' golos'].

The story itself is hilarious – an encyclopaedia of cultural reference, a kind of mini-guide to Russian cultural history. Racing through the gallery, Maiakovsky now resurrects a number of characters depicted in other paintings: the eponymous Cossacks of Ilya Repin's famous painting *Zaporozhian Cossacks Write a Letter to the Turkish Sultan* (1890–1891), the famous pilot Valeri Chkalov, some Soviet marshals, Vissarion Belinsky, Alexander Pushkin, 'some smiling girls…collective farm workers', and – 'Jesus Christ himself'! As the motley crew parades through the gallery, the poet continues to recite: 'Live! Labour! To your last nerve, your last breath! […] I stride into the world, like an indefatigable agitator, to keep singing, on into the future…'

It is tempting to read this sequence as a sly comment on art and politics – and on the increasingly restrictive cultural climate of the late 1940s. Maiakovsky – the original 'Revolutionary' voice of early Bolshevism – is a force of energy, aiming to shake up the Soviet cultural world, to reinvigorate the Revolutionary dream. Through him, the 'eternal agitator', Medvedkin affirms his own belief in agitation, his commitment to political cinema. He, like Maiakovsky, will continue to 'sing', even in this difficult climate.

Such optimism was ill-founded, however. For, as we know, Medvedkin never found the same voice again, and had to sing instead 'in a different voice'. *A Song about the Future* shows how his satiric impulse had no place in the restrictive climate of the late 1940s; its emphasis on perpetual agitation evoked a different cultural climate, in which the experimentation and hyperbole of his earlier work had a more obvious place. In its focus on Maiakovsky, moreover, it may offer us a key to understanding Medvedkin himself, for that uncompromising poet was a figure who had much in common with our hero.[45] He too was a committed Bolshevik, an artist whose dream was to harness his creativity to the building of the new world. He too found his work restricted and challenged by the regime. Maiakovsky committed suicide in 1930, however; Medvedkin lived on until 1989, until the death of that regime itself.

In interview with Marker, Marina Goldovskaya described that first 'Revolutionary' generation of committed artists (Maiakovsky, Vertov, Medvedkin…) as having 'too much feeling, and not enough brain'. For her, this begins to explain the troubling discrepancy between Medvedkin's artistic brilliance and his apparently unquestioning subscription to Soviet ideology. As *The Accursed Force* revealed, Medvedkin's Revolutionary drive was one of 'feeling', of 'spontaneity', a belief in 'revolt'. He was a Bolshevik, rather than a communist, and the Revolution was his foundation; on 7 November 1976 he recorded a celebratory note to himself: 'October is 59 years old today!!'[46] On his eighty-fifth birthday he received a postcard from his old comrade Nikolai Karmazinsky 'to the cavalry solider A. Medvedkin…always in battle, always scouting'.[47]

Karmazinsky was right, for Medvedkin never relinquished his battle. In 1986 he said:

> I feel sincerely sorry for those privileged youths, who waste their best years on fashionable glad rags, disks, dachas, cars. What do they really have left? An emptiness in their heart. The poet [Alexander Blok] spoke the truth when he said that there is a thrill in battle. If you're forbidden to do something useful, socially important, and you manage to do it all the same. They don't let you in the door – you go through the window. The good life is a fight![48]

Here, perhaps, lies the key. Medvedkin's creative life was indeed a fight: a fight with the authorities, and a fight with himself. Drawn in one direction by his politics (his diehard commitment to the project of Soviet socialism) and in another by his art (his recklessly exuberant, excessive, ironic gaze), Medvedkin was at once a servant of the Revolution and its most telling satirist. His early films were an attempt to bring the two sides of his art together, to create a new form of Revolutionary art. In his later career he was forced to acknowledge the impossibility of this project. It is no accident that so many of his films, and his screenplays, turn their gently mocking gaze on those for whom ideas matter more than actions. Duren, the original bureaucrat, reappears in many guises. And it was with bureaucrats just like him that Medvedkin struggled throughout his career.

During the 1970s Medvedkin appears to have suffered from periodic depression.[49] In his diary on 26 October 1976, for example, he wrote of depression 'hindering' his work. The sources of that depression are hinted at in a letter that he wrote to Filipp Ermash, head of the State Committee of Cinema Affairs (Goskino), in 1973. The letter was a plea, once again, for *The Accursed Force*. But it was much more than that – a revealing expression of the director's frustration.

> As a director I was born in Mosfilm. Twice I have been Secretary of the Party organisation here (during the most difficult years). Here I made my best comedies, *Happiness* and *The Miracle Worker*. Today I, like a foreigner or a member of a national minority [*natsman*], am excluded from the working circle, although no one can justify that action by a lack of capability or professional worth, and I turned to documentary film during the difficult period of 'film hunger', so as not to be sitting idle during the difficult post-war years. Help me, Filipp Timofeevich! We have few comedies because in art there is nothing, and never will be anything more difficult than film comedy, and in the end, to throw out comedy is improvident![50]

This beseeching cry comes from the heart, revealing the tragic duality at the centre of Medvedkin's career – the betrayal of his beliefs and dreams. It reveals the full complexity of the figure that Marker honours with such insightful affection in his film, and whose astonishing legacy is with us today in his greatest feature films, his ironic eye giving a knowing but affectionate wink at a difficult century.

Notes

Introduction

1   Chris Marker, 'Kino-medved', introduction to '"Mozhet byt', my rano zagnali v tupik nash poezd?"' Iz perepiski Aleksandra Medvedkina i Krisa Markera', *Kinovedcheskie zapiski*, no. 49, pp.30–82 (32). This is part of a section devoted to Medvedkin, 'Medvedkinu-100', pp.21–147.
2   Alexander Medvedkin, 'Satira – oruzhie atakuiushchego', unpublished manuscript. In the Medvedkin archive in the Museum of Cinema, Moscow (hereafter MC): 1/1/11, p.17.
3   Medvedkin, 'Razdum'ia', *Dokumental noe kino segodnia*, Moscow, 1963, pp.16–28 (16).
4   Medvedkin, 'Razdum'ia', p.16.
5   Medvedkin, 'Razdum'ia', p.21.
6   Rostilav Iurenev, *Medvedkin – Satirik*, Moscow, 1981.
7   Aleksandr Deriabin, 'Ves' Medvedkin: filmografiia', *Kinovedcheskie zapiski*, no. 49, pp.86–115.
8   N. A. Izvolov, 'A. Medvedkin i traditsiia rannego russkogo kino,' *Fenomen kino: Istoriia i teoriia*, Moscow, 2001, pp.229–250.
9   *Le Bonheur* (reprint: ARTE, ZZ Production, le Forum des images); *Happiness* is available on VHS from Kino. For the Russian Cinema Council DVD project, see www.ruscico.com.

Chapter 1

1   MC 1/1/138.
2   Medvedkin, 'Konarmeiskie budni', unpublished manuscript; MC 1/3/130, p.5.
3   Richard Taylor, 'Interview with Alexander Medvedkin', in *Inside the Film Factory: New Approaches to Russian and Soviet Cinema*, Taylor and Ian Christie (eds), London, 1991, pp.165–175 (166). This is a reduced version of a longer interview,

the full transcript of which has kindly been made available to me. In subsequent references, I will refer to the two versions separately.

4   Medvedkin, 'Satira – oruzhie', p.13.

5   Medvedkin, 'Satira – oruzhie', p.2.

6   Medvedkin, 'Konarmeiskie budni', p.5.

7   Interview with Richard Taylor, full transcript, p.4. Medvedkin describes the performance at some length to Marker in *The Last Bolshevik*.

8   Taylor, full transcript, p.4.

9   MC 1/1/140.

10   MC 1/3/62.

11   MC 1/1/147. Diary entry for 23 September 1928.

12   In the archive there are copies of several papers that Medvedkin wrote during this time, focusing on the current state of the film industry's readiness for war, and exploring its potential as a military aid in that event. See, for example, MC 1/1/117. This (undated) paper shows extensive research, and is particularly remarkable for its use of pre-Revolutionary sources. Izvolov, 'A. Medvedkin', pp.231–232, cites other essays of this kind from the archive to prove Medvedkin's unusual interest in pre-Revolutionary precedent.

13   From documents in the archive, it seems that Gosvoenkino's cinematographic training was largely 'on the job', and may have involved courses organised by 'Komsomolkino' (a training for young people in the basics of film-making), documents relating to which Medvedkin later inserted in a file with the heading 'Important: Towards Autobiography!' that he prepared for Harvard University Press during the 1970s. 'Kino-shkoly pri kino', organised by Grisenko, Chaursky and Bolshintsov; MC 1/3/109.

14   See Richard Taylor, *Film Propaganda: Soviet Russia and Nazi Germany*, London, 1998, pp.34–35, for discussion of the short genres used for film propaganda during the 1920s.

15   Medvedkin, 'Gigiena: stsenarii', MC 1/1/2, p.2.

16   Medvedkin, 'Pozitsii ne sdadim', *Proletarskoe kino*, no. 9, 1931, pp.16–19 (17).

17   Denise Youngblood, *Movies for the Masses: Popular Cinema and Soviet Society in the 1920s*, Cambridge, 1992, pp.50–67, provides figures that reveal the importance of foreign films in the Soviet cinema repertoire during the 1920s, and offers an account of the debates that surrounded them.

18   Okhlopkov is best known for his role as Alexander Nevsky in Eisenstein's 1938 masterpiece of that name. During the 1930s he ran the Realistic Theatre in Moscow, where he experimented with devices for overcoming the divide between stage and audience.

19   MC 1/1/1:1. The screenplay of last reel of the film was published in *Sovetskii ekran*, 1 January 1929. The film was reviewed by Herbert Marshall in *Close Up*, no. 5, 1930, pp.332–333. Marshall recounted that he had seen the film in private, and discussed it with Okhlopkov: 'He tells me that some of it is not clear to the Workers, it is his mistake, so he must simplify.' Marshall was very positive about the film.

20   Interview with Martin Walsh and Kate Betz, Richard Taylor (trans.) (unpublished manuscript), p.12.

21   The group consisted of Vladimirsky, Iudin, Gindiny, Afonin, Serpukhovitin, Maslatsov and Zinov'ev.

22   'Novaia fil'ma Medvedkina: Duren' ty, duren'', *Kino*, 16 June 1931, p.3. The article praised Medvedkin's economy.

23   Medvedkin, 'Pozitsii ne sdadim', p.18.
24   Medvedkin, 'Satira – oruzhie', p.15.
25   Taylor, full transcript, p.5.
26   The screenplays for some of these short films are published in Medvedkin, 'Kinofel'etony', in *Iz istorii kino: dokumenty i materialy*, Moscow, 1974, pp.61–86.
27   See Richard L. Chapple, *Soviet Satire of the Twenties*, University of Florida Monographs: Humanities no. 47, 1980, pp.7–82, for discussion of the figure of the bureaucrat in Soviet literary satire.
28   See Thomas Seifrid, *Andrei Platonov: Uncertainties of Spirit*, Cambridge, 1992, for detailed discussion of *The Foundation Pit*.
29   The French comic Max Linder was extremely popular during the pre-Revolutionary period. See Youngblood, *The Magic Mirror: Moviemaking in Russia, 1908–1918*, Madison, 1999, and *Movies for the Masses* for discussion of the popularity of imported films during the pre-Revolutionary and the Soviet periods. During the early 1920s Chaplin enjoyed an almost mythical status among Soviet Revolutionary film-makers. In 1922, for example, the avant-garde journal *Kinofot* published an issue dedicated to Chaplin, illustrated by Varvara Stepanova.
30   V. Blium, 'Vozroditsia li satira', *Literaturnaia gazeta*, 29 June 1929.
31   Cited in R. Iurenev, *Sovetskaia kinokomediia*, Moscow, 1964, p.181.
32   Among Maiakovsky's writings on satire are V. Maiakovskii, 'Mozhno lil stat' satirikom', *Polnoe sobranie sochinenii v 13 tomakh*, Moscow, 1959, t. 12, pp.30–32, and 'Nekotorye sprashivaiut', p.199.
33   Belinsky, 'Thoughts and Notes on Russian Literature', in *Belinsky, Chernyshevsky, Dobroliubov: Essential Writings by the Founders of Russian Literary and Social Criticism*, Ralph Matlaw (ed.), Bloomington, IN, 1976, pp.3–33 (3).
34   Friedrich Ermler, *The Parisian Cobbler* [Parizhskii sapozhnik, 1927] and *Katka's Reinette Apples* [Kat'ka-bumazhnyi ranet, 1929]; Boris Barnet, *Girl with a Hatbox* [Devushka s korobkoi, 1927] and *The House on Trubnaia Square* [Dom na Trubnoi, 1929].
35   See Julian Graffy, *Bed and Sofa*. Kinofile Companion no. 5, London, 2001.
36   Medvedkin, 'Satira – oruzhie', p.15.
37   The first meeting, to discuss the first three short films *Poleshko, Stop Thief* and *Fruit and Vegetables*, was held on 18 December 1930. Present were Skorokhodov, Mikhailov, Kiva, Medvedkin, Iudin, Stepanov, Feldman, Room, Tsukker and Vladimirsky: 'Protokol soveshcheniia po obsuzhdeniiu trekh korotkometrazhek rezh. Medvedkina; MC 1/2/24:3. The second, to discuss the two longer films, *You're Stupid, Mr Stupid* and *About a White Bull-Calf*, was held in June 1931; MC 1/2/121.
38   'Protokol', December 1930, p.3.
39   'Basni Medvedkina: Nuzhny li nam iumor i satira?'; V. Al'tshuler, 'Duren' ty, duren', ili spisok oshibok i dostizhenii Medvedkina'; 'Kino ili Medvedkino: pomoch' khudozhniku pravil'noi kritikoi', *Kino*, 16 July 1931. The collection of articles was linked to an account of screenings and discussion of the films held in ARRK.
40   'Protokol', June 1931, p.9. Lunacharsky linked Medvedkin's work with that of the nineteenth-century satirical writer Mikhail Saltykov-Shchedrin (1826–1889). For Lunacharsky, the skill of Saltykov-Shchedrin lay in its clearly articulated target: 'We need Shchedrin-esque satire, we need to be able to focus.'
41   V. Al'tshuler, p.3.

42   'Kino ili Medvedkino', p.3.
43   Lunacharskii, 'Kinematograficheskaia komediia i satira', *Proletarskoe kino*, no. 9, 1931, pp.4–15 (15).
44   Taylor, full transcript, p.4.
45   'O putiakh razvitiia kratkometrazhnykh fil'm: Rezoliutsiia', MC 1/1/120.
46   Medvedkin, 'Pozitsii', p.18.
47   'Protokol', p.1.
48   See R. Taylor and I. Christie (eds), *The Film Factory: Russian and Soviet Cinema in Documents, 1896–1939*, London, 1988, pp.278–279, for further detail.
49   Sutyrin, 'O sovetskoi satire' (record of speech at ARRK), *Proletarskoe kino*, nos. 10–11, 1930, pp.4–15 (5).
50   In interview with Richard Taylor in 1988, Medvedkin acknowledged the influence of folklore on his early theatrical performances. See Taylor, 'Interview with Alexander Medvedkin', pp.166–167.
51   See Victoria Bonnell, *Iconography of Power: Soviet Political Posters under Lenin and Stalin*, Berkeley, CA, 1997, pp.199–201, and Stephen White, *The Bolshevik Poster*, New Haven, CT, 1988, p.67.
52   In a later interview, however, rather than acknowledging Meyerhold's influence on his work, Medvedkin emphasised a confluence of ideas between himself and the great director. Meyerhold's declaration of war on traditional theatre, he said, echoed his own declaration of war on cinema, and the desire to 'turn the old cinema on its head' (interview with Walsh and Betz, p.12). This would appear unjust to the chronology of the two mens' careers: by the time Medvedkin began his work in cinema – or, indeed, in the army theatre – Meyerhold had been long established. In Medvedkin's lists of self-improving works to read 'on art', scribbled in his diary in September 1928, we find two works devoted to Vsevolod Meyerhold, MC 1/1/147. Diary entry for 23 September 1928.
53   Sergei Eisenstein, 'The Montage of Attractions,' in *The Film Factory*, pp.87–89.
54   Medvedkin, 'Konarmeiskie budni', p.6.
55   Medvedkin, 'Konarmeiskie budni', p.6. Given that American comic films were widely distributed in metropolitan Russia between 1915 and 1930, this claim must be viewed as spurious. It is possible, however, that Medvedkin's upbringing in the provincial town of Penza kept him sheltered from this most virulent of imports.
56   Interview with Walsh and Betz, p.15.
57   Interview with Walsh and Betz, p.16.
58   Medvedkin, 'Pozitsii', p.18.

Chapter 2

1   Medvedkin, '294 dnia na kolesakh', in *Iz istorii kino: dokumenty i materialy*, Moscow, 1977, pp.32–57 (43).
2   Medvedkin first put forward the idea of the film-train in a letter to the director of Soiuzkino, Comrade Markichev, dated 15 July 1930; MC 1/3/120.
3   Medvedkin, 'Chto takoe kinopoezd', in *Iz istorii kino: dokumenty i materialy*, Moscow, 1985, pp.27–62 (28).
4   Interview with Richard Taylor, full transcript, p.6.
5   Medvedkin, '294 dnia na kolesakh', p.54. Also, 'Chto takoe kinopoezd?', p.36.

6   Medvedkin had done his research: in the archive we find annotated pre-
    Revolutionary texts with detailed drawings of carriages, engines – and even
    peculiarly shaped 'railwaymen'; MC 1/2/30.
7   See Deriabin, 'Kinopoezd Soiuzkinokhroniki (1932–1935): Katalog fil'mov',
    Kinovedcheskie zapiski, no. 49, pp.118–144, for a full list of members of the train,
    and of films produced.
8   Nikolai Karmazinsky (1909–198?) had made two travelogues, *Spring Feuilleton*
    [Vesennii fel'eton, 1929], and *Towards the White Hole of the Arctic* [K belomu
    piatnu Arktiki, 1931]. He went on to make many film periodicals and
    newspapers, and shot individual documentaries.
9   Medvedkin, '294 dnia na kolesakh', p.35.
10 Interview with Walsh and Betz, p.10.
11 Medvedkin, 'Chto takoe kinopoezd?', p.28.
12 Medvedkin, 'Plan razvertyvaniia raboty v Krivorozh'e', 31 March 1932; MC
    1/1/120.
13 Medvedkin, 'Chto takoe kinopoezd?', p.32.
14 Medvedkin, 'Chto takoe kinopoezd?', p.28.
15 Medvedkin, '294 dnia na kolesakh', p.36.
16 Medvedkin, 'Chto takoe kinopoezd?', p.30.
17 Although the film has not been preserved, the screenplay for *Pro liubov* is in the
    archive; MC 1/1/19.
18 In the folktale, Ivanushka-durachok (Ivan the Fool) is often the third son. His
    foolishness acts as a form of guarantee of his purity, in a secular version of the
    religious tradition of the *iurodyvyi*, or Holy Fool. See, for example, the tale
    'Letuchii korabl', in *Russkie narodnye skazki: iz sbornika A. N. Afanas'eva*, St
    Petersburg, 1994, pp.180–183, in which it is made explicit that 'God loves fools',
    helping the third son to win the hand of a princess, and to gain wisdom. The
    lazy/foolish son is a recurrent figure in many different kinds of tale, and may carry
    different names, but the appellation 'Ivan' is commonly used in popular parlance
    to refer to the type.
19 'Tit: stsenarii', MC 1/1/16.
20 Nikolai Izvolov has done just that, producing a remarkable animated film out of
    Medvedkin's drawings: *Tit, or the Tale of the Big Spoon* [Tit, ili skaz o bol'shoi
    lozhke, 2000]. He has also reconstructed the early satire *Stop Thief* [1999].
21 MC 1/1/155.
22 Medvedkin, 'Chto takoe kinopoezd?', p.57.
23 Medvedkin, '294 dnia na kolesakh', p.37.
24 Medvedkin, 'Chto takoe kinopoezd?', p.33.
25 Medvedkin, 'Chto takoe kinopoezd?', p.29.
26 Medvedkin, '294 dnia na kolesakh', p.37. Izvolov suggests, similarly, that the
    impact of self-recognition on Medvedkin's viewers must have been dramatic,
    blending familiarity with strangeness, recognition with transformation: Izvolov,
    Fenomen kino, p.247.
27 Medvedkin, '294 dnia na kolesakh', p.37. Also 'Chto takoe kinopoezd?', p.34.
28 The drive to create mobile projection facilities, enabling the dissemination of
    propaganda films, had begun shortly after the Revolution. By 1925 there were
    around 1,000 'travelling cinemas' with mobile projectors (*kinoperedvizhniki*)
    active in the Soviet Union, travelling the nation showing Soviet films (especially
    documentaries).

29 Medvedkin, 'V boiakh za satiry', in *Zhizn' v kino: Veterany o sebe i svoikh tovarishchakh*, Moscow, 1971, pp.232–247 (244).
30 *12 udarnykh reisov*, Moscow, 1934, p.29. Louis Althusser suggests that the success of any ruling system is dependent upon the *interpellation* of the individual citizen as subject; Althusser, *Essays on Ideology*, London, 1984. His model is inflected by the psychoanalytic theories of Jacques Lacan: Lacan's 'mirror stage' suggests that the entrance of a child into the 'symbolic' realm, the first stage of which was the recognition of the self as 'other' in the mirror, is the beginning of subjectivity. Similarly, *interpellation* depends on the citizen recognising him or herself as a subject (in the national sense). Jacques Lacan, 'The Mirror Stage as Formative of the Function "I"', in *Ecrits: A Selection*, Alan Sheridan (ed.), London, 1977, pp.1–7.
31 MC 1/1/154.
32 Medvedkin, '294 dnia na kolesakh', p.37.
33 MC 1/1/12.
34 'O semiotike poniatii "styd" i "strakh" v mekhanizme kul'tury', in Iu.M. Lotman, *Semiosfera, Kul'tura i vzryv, vnutri mysliashchikh mirov: stat'i, issledovaniia, zametki*, St Petersburg, 2001, pp.664–666.
35 Medvedkin, '294 dnia na kolesakh', p.37.
36 Medvedkin, 'Chto takoe kinopoezd?', p.59.
37 *Kino*, 24 February 1932, p.1.
38 'Reis v piatiletku', *Kino*, 18 September 1932, p.3.
39 Medvedkin, 'Chto takoe kinopoezd?', p.59.
40 *12 udarnykh reisov*, p.29.

Chapter 3

1 Medvedkin, 'Novoe kachestvo dramaturgii', *Sovetskoe kino*, no. 11, 1933, pp.15–18 (15).
2 Shumiatsky mentioned the film in a speech, published as 'Na poroge novogo proizvodstvennogo goda', *Kino*, 19 December 1933, p.1. The film was also mentioned in E. Orlikova, 'O kolkhoznoi tematike', *Sovetskoe kino*, no. 11, 1933, pp.11–14 (14).
3 These were, however, issues of which he had long been aware: a screenplay of 1930, for a film to be called *Kaput*, aimed to tackle the 'collective farm problem' directly, seeking to persuade the peasant to join the collective farm in a series of episodes, each of which would be 'a blow to the [spectator's] psyche'. In the scenario, we read of a debate about the role of the Russian peasant to 'feed Europe', meet a dappled horse that refuses to move, and see a village of 'horrifying poverty'. Medvedkin, 'Kaput (Agitplakat): Stsenarii', MC 1/1/4.
4 Medvedkin, 'Novoe kachestvo', p.16.
5 Medvedkin discovered that the title had been changed without his knowledge on the film's release on 15 March 1935. 'I'd been ill. I recovered. [...] I didn't object and nobody asked me.' Cited from Taylor, full transcript, p.13. The term 'possessors' (referring to a debate within mediaeval Russian monasticism as to whether monasteries should own and cultivate land [as *stiazhateli* – 'possessors'] or depend on alms [*ne-stiazhateli*]) described the peasant's desire to acquire and safeguard personal property.

6   In the plans for *Kaput* we read of a recalcitrant horse that refuses to move – an image that recurs directly in *Happiness*. The dappled horse was no stranger to Medvedkin's films. It had appeared first in that famous *Meeting of the Horses*, organised for the theatre of the Red Cavalry division.

7   Medvedkin, 'Novoe kachestvo', p.14.

8   Medvedkin, 'Novoe kachestvo', p.14.

9   Medvedkin, 'Novoe kachestvo', p.16.

10   See *Soviet Writers' Congress 1934: The Debate on Socialist Realism and Modernism – Gorky, Radek, Bukharin, Zhdanov and Others*, London, 1977, for details of the full debate.

11   Medvedkin, 'Novoe kachestvo', p.16.

12   Vladimir Propp, *Morphology of the Folktale*, translated by Larence Scott, Austin, 1994, especially chap. 3, and pp.93–96.

13   Medvedkin, 'Novoe kachestvo', p.17.

14   Medvedkin, 'Novoe kachestvo', p.17.

15   V. I. Fomin, *Pravda skazki: kino i traditsii fol'klora*, Moscow, 2001, p.167.

16   Vladimir Propp, 'Folklore and Reality', in *Theory and History of Folklore*, Anatoly Liberman (ed.), Ariadna Y. Martin and Richard P. Martin (trans.), Minneapolis, 1984, pp.16–38 (21).

17   Medvedkin, '*Stiazheteli*. Stsenarii. Pervyi variant', MC 1/1/25, p.1.

18   Viktor Demin, 'Grazhdanin. Boets. Khudozhnik', *Iskusstvo kino*, 1985, pp.3, 104–110.

19   Propp, p.22.

20   Propp, p.25.

21   D.S. Likhachev, 'Khudozhestvennoe vremia v fol'klore', in *Poetika drevnerusskoi literatury*, Leningrad, 1967, pp.224–254 (230).

22   Eisenstein, 'Happiness', in *S.M. Eisenstein: Selected Works*, vol. 3: *Writings 1934–1947*, Richard Taylor (ed.), London, 1996, pp.52–55 (55).

23   Henri Bergson, *Laughter: An Essay on the Meaning of the Comic*, Cloudesley Brereton and Fred Rothwell (trans.), London, 1913, especially pp.18–22, 57–59.

24   Etymologically, the term '*lubok*' seems to refer to the inner layer of wood (*lub*), which provided the basis for woodblock prints. See Neia Zorkaia, *Fol'klor, lubok, ekran*, Moscow, 1994, p.33. In the course of the nineteenth century more complex, multi-framed *lubki* developed into single printed sheets, folded to resemble very short 'books', similar to the English 'chapbook'. For an excellent discussion of the growth of secular popular literature in Russia, see Jeffrey Brooks, *When Russia Learned to Read: Literacy and Popular Literature, 1861–1917*, Princeton, 1985, chap. 3.

25   Medvedkin believed strongly in the value of silent film, and made a speech to that effect in January 1934. A summary of the discussion was printed in *Kino*: 'Pervyi real'nyi plan: preniia po dokladu tov. B. Shumiatskogo', *Kino*, 10 January 1934, p.2.

26   Taylor, full transcript, p.4.

27   See Joanna Hubbs, *Mother Russia*, Bloomington, IN, 1993, for discussion of the feminine myth in Russian culture.

28   See Martin Walsh, 'The Political Joke in *Happiness*', *Screen*, vol. 19, no. 1, Spring 1978, pp.79–89, for astute discussion of this.

29   'Salo na sale' – the equivalent of a dripping sandwich, and an affectingly modest aspiration, circumscribed within the limits of the peasant imagination.

30   Izvolov, *Fenomen kino*, pp.244–245.

31   Demin, p.110.

32   Medvedkin, '*Stiazheteli*: Stsenarii', p.20. The successful (and rapid) realisation of the colour sequence was discussed in an article by B. Petrov in November 1934, when he announced that it had been achieved in three days; B. Petrov, 'Tsvetnoe kino – realnost'', *Kino*, 21 November 1934, p.3. See also Izvolov, 'Aleksandr Medvedkin i traditsii russkogo kino: zametki o stanovlenii poetiki', *Kinovedcheskie zapiski*, no. 49, pp.21–29 (29).

33   See 'Ves' Medvedkin', p.92.

34   Medvedkin, in discussion of his next proposed film, *The Accursed Force*: 'Stenogramma obsuzhdeniia stsenarii t. Medvedkina *Okaiannaia sila*', 7 November 1935, MC 1/1/24:4, p.2.

35   Medvedkin, essay without title, *Kino*, 10 December 1933, p.2.

36   Medvedkin, 'Novoe kachestvo', p.17.

37   Medvedkin, *Kino*, 10 December 1933, p.2.

38   Medvedkin, '*Stiazheteli*', p.2.

39   Demin, p.104.

40   See my *Visions of a New Land: Soviet Film from the Revolution to the Second World War*, New Haven, CT, 2003, for further discussion.

41   Eisenstein, p.54. Medvedkin prepared a longer version of this essay for publication by Harvard University Press, as part of his memoirs: 'Lektsiia prof. S. M. Eizenshteina, no. 16, 13 December 1934, MC 1/3/62.

42   Eisenstein, p.54.

43   Eisenstein, p.52.

44   Sutyrin, 'O sovetskoi satire,' p.12.

45   Medvedkin, '*Stiazheteli*: Stsenarii, pervyi variant', MC 1/1/ 25, p.30.

46   'Potylikha-Templan', *Kino*, 28 November 1993, p.2.

47   Boris Shumiatskii, 'Trudneishii zhanr osvoen', and F. Ermler, 'Kartina raduetsia', *Kino*, 16 December 1934, p.2.

48   Shumiatskii, 'Na poroge', p.1.

49   See the *Pravda* editorial, '*Chapaeva* posmotrit vsia strana', 21 November 1934, p.1. Reprinted as 'The Whole Country is Watching *Chapaev*', in *The Film Factory*, pp.334–335.

50   Medvedkin, 'Biografiia', Op. 3, no. 62.

51   G. Roshal', 'Fol'klor s novykh pozitsii', and B. Petrov, '*Stiazheteli*', *Kino*, 16 February 1935, p.2.

52   'Slushaia dramaturga A. Medvedkina', *Kino*, 10 November 1933, p.2. The meeting was attended by Esfir Shub and Alexander Macheret.

53   Medvedkin, *Kino*, 10 December 1933, p.2.

Chapter 4

1   Shumiatskii, *Kinomatografiia millionov*, Moscow, 1935; extracts in *The Film Factory*, pp.358–369.

2   Richard Taylor, 'Ideology as Mass Entertainment: Boris Shumyatsky and Soviet Cinema in the 1930s', in *Inside the Film Factory*, pp.193–217.

3   Medvedkin, 'V boiakh za satiru', p.247.

4   'Stenogramma obsuzhdeniia stsenarii t. Medvedkina *Okaiannaia sila*', MC 1/2/24:4. This is an account of a meeting held on 7 November 1935 to discuss the proposed film. Published in *Kinovedcheskie zapiski*, no. 57, pp.217–223.

5   Medvedkin, 'V boiakh za satiru', p.247.

6   'Okaiannaia sila: beseda s rezhisserom A. Medvedkinym', Kino, 11 November
     1935, p.2. A shortened version of Medvedkin's speech at this discussion was
     published by Medvedkin in advance of the discussion: 'Moi zamysli', in Kino,
     23 September 1935, p.2.

7   The earliest surviving screenplay of The Accursed Force dates from 1940, although
     there are notes for the original screenplay in a diary of 1935. In this chapter, I
     will be referring to the 1940 version (MC 1/29/1), as published by Marina
     Karaseva: Alexandr Medvedkin, 'Okaiannaia sila: russkaia narodnaia skazka',
     Kinovedcheskie zapiski, no. 57, pp.183–214. For further detail on other versions
     of the screenplay, see Karaseva, 'Okaiannyi stsenarii: neosushchestvelennyi
     zamysel Aleksandra Medvedkina', Kinovedcheskie zapiski, no. 57, pp.176–182.

8   Taylor, full transcript, p.14.

9   Taylor, full transcript, p.13.

10   Taylor, full transcript, p.14.

11   Medvedkin, 'Okaiannaia sila', p.183.

12   N.A. Nekrasov, 'Komu na Rusi zhit' khorosho', in Sobranie sochinenii, vol. 3,
     Moscow, 1965, pp.159–407. During the 1920s, and indeed throughout the Soviet
     period, Nekrasov was much vaunted as a radical and Revolutionary, praised
     for his 'populist' politics (narodnichestvo). See for example, Lunacharskii,
     'Nikolai Alekseevich Nekrasov', in Sobranie sochinenii, vol. 1, Moscow, 1963,
     pp.211–219.

13   MC 1/1/171 (4 April 1935).

14   MC 1/1/171. In addition to Nekrasov, in his early notes on the film, Medvedkin
     lists Cervantes' Don Quixote, Charlie Chaplin and the Soviet satirical duo Il'f and
     Petrov as further influences; MC 1/1/171. These influences are also mentioned
     in a notebook from 1939; MC 1/1/174.

15   'Stenogramma', p.221.

16   'Stenogramma', p.221.

17   See 'The Terrible Bandit Churkin' (1885), in Entertaining Tsarist Russia: Tales,
     Songs, Plays, Movies, Jokes, Adds and Images from Russian Urban Life 1779–1917,
     James von Geldern and Louise McReynolds (eds), Bloomington, IN, 1998,
     pp.221–230.

18   Maxim Gorky, 'Soviet Literature', in Soviet Writers Congress 1934: The Debate
     on Socialist Realism and Modernism, Gor'ky, Radek, Bukharin, Zhdanov, London,
     1977, pp.27–36.

19   Medvedkin, 'Okaiannaia sila', p.188.

20   Medvedkin, 'Okaiannaia sila', p.194.

21   Medvedkin, 'Okaiannaia sila', p.199.

22   After the Second World War, when the social and political problems of
     collectivisation were less urgent, Medvedkin sought to promote the film less as a
     film about the 'rural problem' and more as a contribution to atheist propaganda.
     MC 1/1/29, p.3. See Karaseva, 'Okaiannyi stsenarii', p.180.

23   Medvedkin's picture of hell as a giant bathhouse has its roots in folk tradition.
     The bathhouse is a space for self-cleansing, but it is also, mythically, an un-
     clean space: by popular tradition, if you go to the bathhouse at night you
     must take in a cross, for that is where the demons rest. See Will Ryan, The
     Bathhouse at Midnight: An Historical Survey of Magic and Divination in Russia,
     Stroud, 1999.

24   The devils of Medvedkin's screenplay have much in common with those that people Russian folk tales. These devils are often slightly foolish beings (they can be both black and white); servants of evil, certainly, but without the grandeur of the Christian Satan.

25   Medvedkin, '*Okaiannaia sila*', pp.198–199. This down-to-earth deity seems to step straight from the pages of Soviet satire of the 1920s, a sideswipe at the consolidating bureaucracies of Soviet society, and the system of 'connections' (*blat*): if you know the right people, you can get anywhere, including heaven. This was a common theme in satirical texts of the 1920s in Soviet Russia, treated in Mikhail Bulgakov's short stories and his *Master and Margarita* (1929).

26   Gorky, p.30. Gorky's appropriation of folk culture to an anti-religious cause relied on a much older precedent, in particular on the famous letter of the radical critic Vissarion Belinsky to Nikolai Gogol in 1847. Rejecting Gogol's association of the peasantry with Orthodoxy in his conservative 'Selected Passages from Correspondence with Friends' ['Vybrannye mesta iz perepiski s druz'iami', 1847], Belinsky pointed out that folk culture was often *anti* religious – or, at the very least, that it approached religious questions with a vital realism.

27   'Stenogramma', p.217.

28   'Stenogramma', p.218.

29   See my *Visions of a New Land*, pp.183–189, for further discussion of the shifting images of the village during the 1930s.

30   MC 1/1/174.

31   See Eve Levin, 'Dvoeverie and Popular Religion', in Stephen K. Batalden (ed.), *Seeking God: The Recovery of Religious Identity in Orthodox Russia, Ukraine, and Georgia*, Dekalb, IL, 1993, pp.29–52. This blend of organised religion with pagan tradition is not, of course, unique to Russia; in fact, it is characteristic of what might be called 'rural' belief.

32   'Stenogramma', p.218.

33   Improvements in Russian technology led Medvedkin to believe that these could be realised more successfully than those he had attempted for *Happiness*: 'Stenogramma', p.220.

34   'Stenogramma', p.217.

35   Medvedkin, '*Okaiannaia sila*', p.201. See *Kratkaia entsiklopediia slavianskoi mifologii*, N.S. Shaparova (ed.), Moscow, 2001, p.25.

36   Medvedkin, '*Okaiannaia sila*', p.202.

37   April 1935; MC 1/1/171.

38   Medvedkin, '*Okaiannaia sila*', p.193.

39   Medvedkin, '*Okaiannaia sila*', p.210.

40   Medvedkin, '*Okaiannaia sila*', p.211.

41   Medvedkin planned that the film would be made in two versions: silent, and in sound. The silent version was essential to enable screenings outside major cities, but it is clear that it was envisaged primarily as a sound film. '*Okaiannaia sila*: beseda s rezhisserom A. Medvedkinym', p.2.

42   Medvedkin, '*Okaiannaia sila*', p.213.

43   Katerina Clark, *The Soviet Novel: History as Ritual*, Bloomington, IN, 2000 (first printed Texas, 1981), pp.15–16.

44   Boris Pil'niak, 'Golyi god', in *Izbrannye proizvedeniia*, Moscow, 1976, pp.35–187 (83–86).

45   Clark, pp.15–16.

46   For further reading, see, for example, J. Arch Getty and Oleg V. Naumov (eds), *The Road to Terror: Stalin and the Self-Destruction of the Bolsheviks, 1932–1939*, New Haven, CT, 1999, pp.181–183.

47   Eisenstein, 'Tezisy vystupleniia v zashchitu stsenarii A. Medvedkina *Okaiannaia sila*' (TsGALI, fond 1923, MC 1/1/1403:1, p.145). On 11 January 1940 Medvedkin recorded impressions from a meeting with Eisenstein the previous day, at which they discussed the latest version of *A Blessed Lot* ['Svetlaia dolia', another title for the film]; MC 1/3/64.

48   MC 1/3/14. Medvedkin recounts a screening in Paris of his 1936 film, *The Miracle Worker*, and recording his impressions of the 'inhumane capitalism' of Paris. The note 'I want *The Accursed Force*' appears unconnected, but is underlined. Such notes can be found throughout his diaries.

49   MC 1/1/354:1. As late as 1986, indeed, he had one last hope that the film might be made, when he saw the first film of the young Leningrad director, Sergei Ovcharov. This film, entitled *Nebyval'shchina* [A Fantastic Story, 1989], drew explicitly on folk motifs to offer a modern fable of Ivan the Fool. Ovcharov, Medvedkin thought, was the ideal inheritor of his folkloric-satiric tradition – and of his screenplay. (I am grateful to Nikolai Izvolov for bringing this to my attention.)

50   Medvedkin, 'V boiakh za satiru', p.24.

Chapter 5

1   Medvedkin, '*Chudesnitsa*', *Kino*, 17 August 1936, p.3.

2   Boris Shumiatskii, 'The Film "Bezhin Meadow"', reprinted in *The Film Factory*, pp.378–381.

3   MC 1/1/172.

4   Medvedkin, '*Chudesnitsa*', p.3.

5   Ef. Borisov, 'Organizovannost' i chetkost'', *Kino*, 17 August 1936, p.3.

6   Nikolai Klado, '*Chudesnitsa*', *Kino*, 17 January 1937, p.2.

7   Medvedkin, '*Chudesnitsa*: Komediia', Literaturnaia zapis' montazhnykh listov fil'ma', MC 1/1/25, p.1.

8   M. Shevchenko, 'Na puti k realizmu', *Iskusstvo kino*, no. 2, 1937, pp.48–52 (51).

9   Medvedkin, 'Literaturnaia zapis'', p.42.

10   Medvedkin, 'Literaturnaia zapis'', p.1.

11   Medvedkin, '*Chudesnitsa*', p.3.

12   Medvedkin, 'Literaturnaia zapis'', p.30.

13   Medvedkin, 'Literaturnaia zapis'', p.1.

14   Medvedkin, '*Chudesnitsa*', p.3.

15   Klado, '*Chudesnitsa*', p.2.

16   MC 1/1/172.

17   Klado, '*Chudesnitsa*', p.2.

18   Shevchenko, p.52.

19   Medvedkin, '*Chudesnitsa*', p.3.

20   Medvedkin, 'Literaturnaia zapis'', p.2.

21   MC 1/1/171.

22   Medvedkin, '*Chudesnitsa*', p.3.

23   Medvedkin, 'Literaturnaia zapis'', p.13.

24   MC 1/1/171.
25   Oleg Kovalov, 'Sovetskyi lubok', *Iskusstvo kino*, no. 2, 1993, pp.73–81 (75).
26   Medvedkin, *'Chudesnitsa'*, p.3.
27   Jay Leyda, 'Une autre résurrection', *Ecran*, February 1972, pp.51–52 (52).
28   MC 1/1/171.
29   Medvedkin, *'Chudesnitsa'*, p.3.
30   Medvedkin, *'Chudesnitsa'*, p.3. The same praise of the character, marked out by love of his work, was repeated by Shevchenko, p.50.
31   Klado, p.4.
32   Kovalov, p.75.
33   Citing Maksim Gorky: an intertitle from filmed newspaper *Nashi dostizheniia* (1930).
34   Medvedkin, 'Literaturnaia zapis'', p.3.
35   Shumiatskii, 'Cinema for the Millions', p.368.
36   Klado, p.2.
37   Shevchenko, p.50.
38   A report of the discussion was published: 'Na obsuzhdenii *Chudesnitsy* v Mosfil'me', *Kino*, 11 January 1937, p.2.
39   Shevchenko, p.49.
40   Medvedkin, 'K biografiiu', 22 May 1974; MC 1/3/62, p.4. Visiting Paris in 1977 for a screening of *The Miracle Worker*, he recorded his lack of pleasure in the film, wishing that he had been able to make *The Accursed Force*.
41   Iurenev, *Sovetskaia kinokomediia*, p.286.
42   Demin, 'Medvedkin', in *20 rezhisserskikh biografii*, Moscow, 1971, p.256.
43   Leyda, 'Une autre résurrection', pp.51–52.
44   Kovalov, p.74.
45   Kovalov, p.75.

Chapter 6

1   Leyda, 'Une autre résurrection', p.51.
2   Marcel Martin, 'Propos d'Alexandre Medvedkine: receuillis au magnétophone à Moscou', *Ecran*, February 1972, pp.46–48 (49).
3   Taylor, full transcript, p.15.
4   Medvedkin, *'Veselaia Moskva*: rabochii stsenarii', MC 1/1/28:2, pp.131–211 (151). *Jolly Moscow* was the film's working title.
5   For discussion of the status of Moscow in the culture of the 1920s and 1930s, see my *Visions of a New Land*, pp.164–183.
6   Klado, *'Veselaia Moskva'*, *Kino*, 11 May 1938, p.4.
7   See Graffy, *Bed and Sofa*, for further discussion.
8   See Greg Castillo, 'Gorky Street and the Design of the Stalin Revolution', in *Streets: Critical Perspectives on Public Space*, Zeynip Çelik, Diane Favro and Richard Ingersoll (eds), Berkeley, CA, 1994, pp.57–70.
9   Medvedkin, 'Rabochii stsenarii', p.150.
10   Mikhail Bakhtin, *The Dialogic Imagination: Four Essays by Mikhail Bakhtin*, Michael Holquist (ed.), Austin, TX, 1981, p.212.
11   Medvedkin uses the winning design of Iofan and Gelfreich for this representation. See Alexei Tarkhanov and Sergei Kavtaradze, *Architecture of the Stalin Era*, New York, 1992, pp.25–38, for further discussion of the Palace of the Soviets.

12   Vadim Alisov, 'Semeinaia relikviia', *Iskusstvo kino*, no. 8, 1997, pp.34–37.
13   Oksana Bulgakova, 'Sorevnovanie kinofantazii', in *Berlin-Moskva: Teatr, Literatura, Musyka, Kino*, Munich, 1996, pp.361–365 (363).
14   *Ocherki istorii sovetskogo kino*, tom 2, Moscow, 1959, pp.236–237.
15   Evgenii Margolit and Viacheslav Shmyrov, *Iz"iatoe kino: katalog sovestskikh igrovykh kartin, ne vypushchennykh vo vsesoiuznyi prokat po zavershenii v proizvodstve ili iz"iatykh iz deistvuiushchego fil'mofonda v god vypuska na ekran (1924–1953)*, Moscow, 1995, pp.63–64 (64).
16   The similarities between *New Moscow* and Pyrev's 1941 film do not end there: the figure of the female swineherd appears in both films, and Margolit and Shmyrov (1995) point out the similarity in the lyrics between the two songs of praise to Moscow.
17   Klado, '*Veselaia Moskva*', p.4.
18   G. Ermolaev, 'What is Holding Up the Development of Soviet Cinema?', reprinted in *The Film Factory*, pp.386–387.
19   Dukelsky was removed from his post in mid-1939 and replaced by Ivan Bolshakov, who remained in the post into the post-war period (named Minister of Cinema in 1946).
20   G. Ryklin, '*Novaia Moskva*: proizvod'stvo kinostudii 'Mosfil'm'', *Pravda*, 7 January 1939, p.4. Another review was published in *Izvestiia*, 9 January 1939.
21   Ryklin, p.4.
22   Iurenev, *Aleksandr Medvedkin*, p.41.

Chapter 7

1   'Na tribune – mastera kino', *Vecherniaia Moskva*, 17 August 1939, p.3.
2   Karaseva, 'Okaiannyi stsenarii', p.179.
3   *Vecherniaia Moskva*, 9 July 1939, p.3. The film (using chromide gelatine colour technology) was completed by September.
4   Official Order dated 15 November 1941; MC 1/2/10:2.
5   Peter Kenez, *Cinema and Soviet Society: From the Revolution to the Death of Stalin*, London, 2001, p.169.
6   MC 1/1/134, June 1944.
7   Medvedkin, 'Podgotovka kino-promyshlennosti k voine', MC 1/1/117.
8   Medvedkin, 'Dokladnaia zapiska: O sozdanii avto-kino-bazy', MC 1/1/121. Also 10 June 1944, MC 1/1/122.
9   MC 1/2/12:1–2.
10   MC 1/3/46.
11   In February 1945 his work at the front was assessed by military command, and he was judged to have shown 'initiative, energy, and good leadership skills'; MC 1/2/10:1.
12   Medvedkin, ''Soldat snimaet kino', in *Ikh oruzhie – kinokamera*, Moscow, 1984, pp.246–250.
13   Although Medvedkin later complained that the film was never 'his', it seems clear from the archive that he integrated ideas for a film that he had had as early as 1943. Among his documents, there is a drawn screenplay for a film to be entitled *The Return* [Vozvrashchenie], which shares many elements with the final version of *The Liberated Land*; MC 1/1/83.

14   The letter is dated 18 July; MC 1/4/4.

15   MC 1/4/7, 31 July 1946.

16   Cited in Kenez, pp.195–196.

17   G. Borodin, '*Skoraia pomoshch*': iz istorii mul'tfil'ma Medvedkina', *Kino-vedcheskie zapiski*, no. 49, pp.83–85.

18   MC 1/1/54:2.

19   'Prikaz Ministerstva Kinematografii SSSR', 28 March 1949; *Kinovedcheskie zapiski*, no. 49, pp.84–85. Reprint of document from RGALI: f. 2469, MC 1/1/18.

20   Alexander Prokhurov, 'The Unknown New Wave: Soviet Cinema of the 1960s', in *Springtime for Soviet Cinema: Re/Viewing the 1960s*, Alexander Prokhurov (ed.), Pittsburgh, 2001, pp.7–28 (8). See *Kinematograf ottepeli: dokumenty i svidedet'stva*, Valerii Fomin (ed.), Moscow, 1998, for extensive documentation of the politics and practices of this period; also V. Fomin, *Kino i vlast': Sovetskoe kino 1965–1985 gody*, Moscow, 1996. Josephine Woll, *Real Images: Soviet Cinema and the Thaw*, London, 2000, provides an excellent overview of this period.

21   Evgenii Margolit, 'Landscape, with hero,' in *Springtime for Soviet Cinema*, pp.29–50 (34).

22   Medvedkin, 'Biografiia', p.5.

23   Medvedkin, 'Biografiia', p.5.

24   Medvedkin, 'Razdum'ia', p.24.

25   MC 1/1/4.

26   Demin, p.110.

27   Thus he followed the example of Esfir Shub, whose well-known films, including *The Fall of the Romanovs* [Padenie dinastii Romanovykh, 1927], similarly consisted of re-edited footage.

28   'Kinopoezd otpravliaetsia v sovremennost' (beseda M. Kanevskogo s A.I. Medvedkinym)', *Sovetskaia kul'tura*, 7 November 1979, p.6.

29   MC 1/1/76.

30   MC 1/1/86.

31   Letter dated 4 April 1968, 'Iz perepiski Aleksandra Medvedkina i Krisa Markera', p.33.

32   23 November 1985; MC 1/3/85:20 and MC 1/3/85:9.

33   MC 1/3/66.

34   Margolit, '"Kinematograf ottepeli": k portretu fenomena', *Kinovedcheskie zapiski*, no. 61, pp.195–231 (216).

35   *Le monde*, 2 December 1971. It is interesting that Marker felt the need to publish a note pointing out that Medvedkin was a proud and happy citizen of the Soviet Union. Rebutting claims that Medvedkin had not been allowed to travel to Paris to attend the screening of *Happiness* in 1971, he wrote: 'Can it be that in the eyes of some a Soviet citizen is only interesting in the extent to which he can be used against his country?'

36   'Iz perepiski Aleksandra Medvedkina i Krisa Markera', pp.30–82.

37   23 January 1970; MC 1/1/304.

38   Dated 9 July 1969; MC 1/1/94:8.

39   Other articles in the French press include *Politique*, 2 December 1971; *Journal du Dimanche*, 5 December 1971; *Humanité*, 1 December 1971; and *Nouvel observateur*, 19 November 1971. In the English press, *Cineaste*, vol. 5, no. 2, Spring 1972, and *Time Out*, 7 December 1973 (premiere). At a recent retrospective of the work of Jean-Luc Godard, in July 2002, the British Film Institute named Medvedkin as

'a clear precursor to Godard in his mixture of "high" and "low" narrative film styles for the propagation of revolutionary thought'.

40   MC 1/1/297.
41   MC 1/1/14.
42   MC 1/1/14.
43   'Iz perepiski Aleksandra Medvedkina i Krisa Markera', 19 January 1989, p.82.
44   MC 1/1/52. See also Iurenev, p.48.
45   I am grateful to Julian Graffy for this interesting observation.
46   MC 1/1/12.
47   MC 1/1/308:2. Karmazinsky uses a term, *razvedka* ('scouting', 'exploration'), common during the First Five-Year Plan, in reference to his and Medvedkin's shared adventure on the film-train, implicitly acknowledging this as a golden period in the life of this soldier-film-maker.
48   '"Kompromissov ne priznaiu": Beseda s interesnym chelovekom', *Leninskoe znamia*, 20 June 1985, p.3. A discussion between Medvedkin and G. Mylnikova.
49   MC 1/3/87, p.3. Now an old man, he was also frequently ill; by the time his wife Vera died in 1985 he himself had had four minor strokes.
50   MC 1/2/29.

Filmography

This is not a complete list of films directed by Alexander Medvedkin; a complete filmography (of the director, and of all the films produced on the film-train) has been published in *Kinovedcheskie zapiski*, no. 49. Here I list all the films referred to in the text, and selected other features and documentaries. For the film-train films not directed by Medvedkin, see also *Kinovedcheskie zapiski*.

Explorations [Razvedki, 1927]
Gosvoenkino
Script: A.I. Medvedkin
Film not preserved

Floodlight [Prozhektor, 1929]
Gosvoenkino
Script: A.I. Medvedkin
Director: N.P. Okhlopkov
Director of photography: Ya.M. Tolchan
Film not preserved

Look After Your Health [Beregi zdorov'e, 1929]
Gosvoenkino
Director: A.I. Medvedkin
Director of photography: V.V. Solovev
Film partially preserved in Rossiiskii gosudarstvennyi arkhiv kinofotodokumentov
(RGAKFD), archive no. 3584

The Way of the Enthusiasts [Put' entuziastov, 1930]
Sovkino
Script: G.I. Pavliuchenko, N.P. Okhlopkov
Director: N.P. Okhlopkov
Director of photography: M.I. Vladimirsky
Design: V.P. Komardenkov
Assistant director: A.I. Medvedkin
Cast

Worker	N.V. Sibiriak
Red Army accordionist	V.A. Maslatsov
Peasant	V. Panasiuk
	N.I. Orlov

Film not preserved

Stop Thief [Derzhi vora, 1930]
Soiuzkino
Script and director: A.I. Medvedkin
Director of photography: M.I. Vladimirovsky
Cast

Petty thief	V.A. Maslatsov
Blundering tractor driver	A.I. Medvedkin
Old watchman	K. Gun

Film not preserved

Fruit and Vegetables [Frukty-ovoshchi, 1930]
Soiuzkino
Script and director: A.I. Medvedkin
Director of photography: M.I. Vladimirovsky
Assistant directors: M. Afonin, G. Serpukhovitin
Film not preserved

Poleshko [1930]
Soiuzkino
Script and director: A.I. Medvedkin
Director of photography: M.I. Vladimirovsky
Assistant directors: M. Afonin, G. Serpukhovitin
Film not preserved
Cast

House painter	V.A. Maslatsov

About a White Bull-Calf [Pro belogo bychka, 1931]
Soiuzkino
Script and director: A.I. Medvedkin
Director of photography: M.E. Gindin
Design: A.A. Utkin
Cast

V.A. Maslatsov and others
Film not preserved

You're Stupid, Mr Stupid [Duren' ty, duren', 1931]
Script and director: A.I. Medvedkin
Director of photography: N.K. Yudin
Design: D.A. Kolupaev
Cast
Engineer Ivan Ivanovich Duren'   P.A. Zinov'ev
Film not preserved

Kino-gazeta no. 2 [1932]
Kinopoezd Soiuzkinokhroniki
Director: A.I. Medvedkin
Director of photography: G.A. Troiansky
Film not preserved

Kino-gazeta no. 3 [1932]
Kinopoezd Soiuzkinokhroniki
Director: A.I. Medvedkin
Photography: A.L. Bogorov, G.A. Troiansky, V.N. Maslennikov
Film not preserved

A Camel Visits the Dnepropetrovsk Steam Locomotive Repair Works [Puteshestvie
verbliuda na Dnepropetrovskom parovozoremontnom zavode], aka *Camel at the PRZ*
[Verbliud na PRZ, 1932]
Script: A.I. Medvedkin
Animators: Kochergin, Iu. Popov, Rostovtsev
Editor: G.K. Piotrovsky
Directors of photography: D.I. Karetny (animation), V.N. Maslennikov (live action)
Film not preserved

About Love [Pro Liubov', 1932]
Kinopoezd Soiuzkinokhroniki
Director: A.I. Medvedkin
Director of photography: G.A. Troiansky
Animator: V.I. Polkovnikov
Cast
Volodia the haulier   V.A. Maslatsov
Olia   O. Tsapkina
Film not preserved

The Hole [Dyra, 1932]
Kinopoezd Soiuzkinokhroniki
Director: A.I. Medvedkin
Director of photography: G.A. Troiansky
Assistant director: B.M. Mitiakin
Cast
Tiukhin, collective farmer and water carrier   V.A. Maslatsov
Film not preserved

Tit [1932]
Kinopoezd Soiuzkinokhroniki
Script and director: A.I. Medvedkin
Director of photography: G.A. Troiansky
Assistant director: B.M. Mitiakin
Cast
Tit   V.A. Maslatsov
Film not preserved

Kino-gazeta no. 16 [1932]
Kinopoezd Soiuzkinokhroniki
Director: N.N. Karmazinsky
Photography: A.I. Medvedkin, G.A. Troiansky
Film not preserved

The Trap [Zapodnia], aka *The Unusual Adventures of the Artillery Supervisor*
[Neobyknovennye prikliucheniia artilleriiskogo nabliudatel'ia] or *The Daring Lad*
[Likhoi paren', 1932]
Kinopoezd Soiuzkinokhroniki
Script and director: A.I. Medvedkin
Director of photography: G.A. Troiansky
Assistant director: B.M. Mitiakin
Cast
Red Army man   V.A. Maslatsov
Enemy soldier   D.I. Karetny
Film not preserved

Steel [Stal'], aka *On Good and Bad Steel* [O khoroshei i negodnoi stali, 1932–1933]
Director: A.I. Medvedkin
Director of photography: G.A. Troiansky
Film not preserved

Happiness [Schast'e, 1935]
Moskinokombinat
Script and director: A.I. Medvedkin
Director of photography: G.A. Troiansky
Design: A.A. Utkin
Cast
Khmyr'   P.A. Zinov'ev
Anna, Khmyr''s wife   E.G. Egorova
Nun   L. Nenasheva
B. Uspensky, G. Mirgorian, V. Lavrentev
Preserved in Gosfilmofond of Russia

The Miracle Worker [Chudesnitsa, 1936]
Mosfilm
Script and director: A.I. Medvedkin
Director of photography: I.V. Gelein
Design: I.I. Meden
Composer: L.A. Shvarts
Cast

Zinka the miraculous girl, a milkmaid	Z.A. Bokareva
Ivan, a shepherd	S.N. Bulaevsky
Maliutka, a milkmaid	V.E. Smetana-Tolstova
Varvara	E.S. Ibragimova-Dobrzhanskaia
Matvei, head of collective farm	L.A. Alexeev
Savva, hairdresser	Z.A. Sazhin
Ul'iana, the last witch	M.V. Shlenskaia
Nikolai Stepanovich, captain	I.V. Shtraukh
Public prosecutor	K. Gun
Dentist	V. Shtraus
Slow firewarden	L. Ivanov

Songs performed by the Piatnitsky Choir
Preserved in Gosfilmofond of Russia

New Moscow [Novaia Moskva, 1938]
Mosfil'm
Script and director: A.I Medvedkin
Director of photography: I.V. Gelein
Co-director: A.B. Olenin
Director of trick cinematography: V.I. Kadochnikov
Composer: V.M. Iurodovsky
Cast

Old woman	M.M. Bliumental-Tamarina
Alesha	D.L. Sagal
Zoia	N.U. Alisova
Olia	M.P. Barabanova
Fedia	A.K. Grave

Preserved in Gosfilmofond of Russia

Blossoming Youth [Tsvetushchaia iunost', 1939]
Lenfil'm and Mosfil'm
Director: A.I. Medvedkin
Second director: V. Feinberg
Assistant: G.A. Kalabanov
Technical director and director of colour photography: F.F. Provorov
Composer: V.Ya. Kruchinin
Preserved in RGAKFD, archive no. 6704

We Await Your Victorious Return [My zhdem vas s pobedoi, 1941]
Mosfilm
Script: A.I. Medvedkin
Directors: A.I. Medvedkin, I.Z. Trauerberg
Photography: K.A. Kuznetsov, T.P. Lebeshev
Cast

Smith	B.I. Chirkov
Female collective farmer	L.N. Smirnova

Preserved in Gosfilmofond of Russia

The Battle for Vitebsk [Srazhenie za Vitebsk, 1944]
TsSDF (Central Studio of Documentary Film)
Director: I.P. Kopalin
Head of film crew at the front line: A.I. Medvedkin
Preserved in RGAKFD, archive no. 5223

Our Minsk [Minsk nash, 1944]
TsSDF
Director: Ya.M. Poselsky
Head of film crew at the front line: A.I. Medvedkin
Preserved in RGAKFD, archive no. 6738

The Liberation of Vilnius [Osvobozhdenie Vil'niusa, 1944]
TsSDF
Director: L.V. Varlamov
Head of film crew at the front line: A.I. Medvedkin
Preserved in RGAKFD, archive no. 5222

In Eastern Prussia [V Vostochnoi Prussii, 1944]
TsSDF
Director and editor: I.P. Kopalina
Head of film crew at the front line: A.I. Medvedkin
Preserved in RGAKFD, archive no. 5157

In the Wolf's Lair (Eastern Prussia): From the Front-line [V logove zveria
(Vostochnaia Prussiia): Frontovoi vypusk, 1945]
TsSDF
Director: Ia.M. Posel'sky
Heads of film crew at the front line: A.I. Medvedkin, M.A. Troianovsky
Preserved in RGAKFD, archive no. 5153

The Liberated Land [Osvobozhdennaia zemlia, 1946]
Sverdlovskaia kinostudiia
Script: Z. Markina, A. Tarasov
Producer: A.I. Medvedkin
Director of photography: Iu. Pazunov
Director: A.A. Dzhaliashvili
Cast

Old man Murliuk	V.V. Vanin
Nadezhda Prituliak	E.V. Tsesarskaia
Kovrygin, head of collective farm	S. Kalinin
Kostenko, head of district soviet	A.L. Khvylia
Foma Ignatievich, agronomist	A. Denisov
Tanka	V.V. Altaiskaia
Daria	N. Dintan
MTS director	A.I. Medvedkin

Preserved in Gosfilmofond of Russia

Emergency Service [Skoraia pomoshch', 1949]
Soiuzmultfilm
Script: A.I. Medvedkin
Director: L. Bredis
Artist: S. Belkovskaia
Director of photography: E. Petrova
Composer: N.I. Peiko
Preserved in Gosfilmofond of Russia

Soviet Tuva [Sovetskaia Tuva, 1951]
TsSDF
Script: E.G. Krigera, A.I. Medvedkin
Director: A.I. Medvedkin
Photography: A.M. Zeniakin, Iu.G Leongardt, N. Solovev, S.Ia. Uralov
Partially preserved in RGAKFD, archive no. 9277

First Spring [Pervaia vesna, 1954]
TsSDF
Directors: I.M. Poselsky, A.I. Medvedkin
Photography: I.D. Grachev, L.P.Zaitsev, A.M. Zeniakin, D.A. Kaspii, S.Ia. Kogan,
A.A. Krylov, V.V. Mikosha, A.I. Sologubov, K.I. Shironin
Preserved in RGAKFD, archive no. 15553

A Spring without Rest [Bespokoinaia vesna, 1956]
Alma-Atinskaia kinostudiia
Script and producer: A.I. Medvedkin
Director of photography: V.N. Maslennikov
Composers: E.G. Brusilovsky, B. B. Baikadamov
Director: S.S. Gruzo
Cast

Zhenia Omega, water carrier and tractor driver	S.S. Gruzo
Olga	R. Shorokhova
Idris, tractor driver	I. Nogaibaev
Raia	N.P. Grebeshkova
Filia, enthusiast	V. Boriskin
Kotik	V. Tiagushev
Borodavka	I. Libyzovsky
Uncle Vasia	G. Fedorovsky

Film preserved in Gosfilmofond of Russia

A Struggle for Billions [Bitva za milliard, 1956]
Alma-Atinskaia kinostudiia
Script: V. Abyzov, V. Savvin (A.I. Medvedkin)
Director: M. Dulepo
Photography: A. Kolesnikov, A. Kulokolov, V. Shcherbatykh, V. Zaitsev, M. Dodonov, O.V. Zekki
Preserved in Tsentral'nyi Gosudarstvennyi arkhiv kinofotodokumentov i zvukozapisei respubliki Kazakhstana, archive no. 1009

Thoughts of Happiness [Dumy o schast'e, 1957]
Alma-Atinskaia kinostudiia
Script and producer: A.I. Medvedkin
Director: K. Abuseitov
Photography: M. Dodonov, A.I. Frolov
Preserved in Tsentral'nyi Gosudarstvennyi arkhiv kinofotodokumentov i zvukozapisei respubliki Kazakhstana, archive no. 1244

Attention! Rockets on the Rhine! [Vnimanie! Rakety na Reine!, 1959]
TsSDF
Script: N. Poliakov, A.I. Medvedkin
Director: A.I. Medvedkin
Preserved in RGAKFD, archive no. 18245

Reason against Madness [Razum protiv bezumiia, 1960]
TsSDF
Script: B. Leontev, A.I. Medvedkin
Director: A.I. Medvedkin
Director of photography: V.M. Usanov
Composer: N.I. Ivanov-Radkevic
Preserved in RGAKFD, archive no. 18688

The Law of Baseness [Zakon podlosti, 1962]
TsSDF
Script and director: A.I. Medvedkin
Photography: N.V. Generalov, A.S. Kochetov, V.I. Khodiakov
Preserved in RGAKFD, archive no. 20081

Dawn of the Republic of Ghana [Utro respubliki Gana, 1963]
TsSDF
Director and author of commentary: A.I. Medvedkin
Director of photography: A.S. Kochetov
Preserved in RGAKFD, archive no. 19091

Peace to Vietnam [Mir V'etnamu, 1965]
TsSDF
Director: A.I. Medvedkin
Preserved in RGAKFD, archive no. 21093

Our Friend Sun Yat-Sen [Nash drug Sun' Iat-sen, 1966]
TsSDF
Script: Iu. Garsh'iantsa, A.I. Medvedkin
Director: A.I. Medvedkin
Photography: G.K. Epifanov, K. Krylova
Preserved in RGAKFD, archive no. 21664

The Forgetful Conscience [Skleroz sovesti, 1968]
TsSDF
Script and director: A.I. Medvedkin
Director of photography: E.I. Efimov
Preserved in RGAKFD, archive no. 24704

Letter to a Chinese Friend [Pis'mo kitaiskomu drugu, 1969]
TsSDF
Script and director: A.I. Medvedkin
Director of photography: E.I. Efimov
Preserved in RGAKFD, archive no. 25045

Night over China [Noch' nad Kitaem, 1971]
TsSDF
Script and director: A.I. Medvedkin
Composer: E.V. Denisov
Preserved in RGAKFD, archive no. 31860

A Chronicle of Alarm [Trevozhnaia khronika, 1972]
TsSDF
Script: A.I. Medvedkin, A. Chepurnov
Director: A.I. Medvedkin
Composer: A.V. Denisov
Preserved in RGAKFD, archive no. 26316

Attention! Maoism! [Ostorozhno! Maoizm!, 1976, re-edited 1979]
TsSDF
Script and director: A.I. Medvedkin
Composer: E.V. Denisov
Preserved in RGAKFD, archive no. 28970 [1976 version], 28726 [1979 version]

Madness [Bezumie, 1979]
TsSDF
Script and director: A.I. Medvedkin
Photography: V.I. Lovkov, L. Kopysov, V. Bukhovtseva
Composer: E.V. Denisov
Preserved in RGAKFD, archive no. 28690

The Alarm [Trevoga, 1984]
Script and director: A.I. Medvedkin
Preserved in RGAKFD, archive no. 30065

Select Bibliography

The following lists only relatively recent critical articles on Medvedkin, and easily available sources. All key contemporary sources are referred to in the notes to the text.

Bibliographical Works, Books and Articles in Russian

Borodin, Georgi, '"Skoraia pomoshch": iz istorii mul'tfil'ma Medvedkina', *Kinovedcheskie zapiski*, no. 49, pp.83–85.

Bulgakova, O., 'Sorevnovanie kinofantazii', in *Berlin-Moscow: Teatr, Literatura, Musyka, Kino*. Munich: Prestel, 1996, pp.361–365.

Demin, Viktor, 'Grazhdanin. Boets. Khudozhnik', *Iskusstvo kino*, no. 3, 1985, pp.103–110.

Demin, Viktor, 'Medvedkin', in *20 rezhisserskikh biografii*. Moscow, 1971, p.256.

Deriabin, Aleksandr, 'Ves' Medvedkin', *Kinovedcheskie zapiski*, no. 49, pp.86–115.

Iurenev, Rostislav, *Aleksandr Medvedkin – Satirik*. Moscow, 1980.

Iurenev, Rostislav, *Sovetskaia kinokomediia*, Moscow, 1964.

Izvolov, Nikolai, 'A. Medvedkin i traditsii rannego russkogo kino', in *Fenomen kino: istoriia i teoriia*, Moscow, 2001.

Karaseva, Marina (ed.), 'Mozhet byt', my rano zagnali v tupik nash poezd?' Iz perepiski Aleksandra Medvedkina i Krisa Markera', *Kinovedcheskie zapiski*, no. 49, pp.30–83.

Karaseva, Marina, 'Okaiannyi stsenarii: neosushchestvlennyi zamysel Aleksandra Medvedkina', *Kinovedcheskie zapiski*, no. 57, pp.176–182.

Kovalov, Oleg, 'Sovetskii lubok', *Iskusstvo kino*, no. 2, 1993, pp.73–81.

Margolit, Evgenii and Viacheslav Shmyrov, *Iz"iatoe kino: katalog sovestskikh igrovykh kartin, ne vypushchennykh vo vsesoiuznyi prokat po zavershenii v proizvodstve ili iz"iatykh iz deistvuiushchego fil mofonda v god vypuska na ekran (1924–1953)*, Moscow, 1995.

Medvedkin, Alexander, 'V boiakh za satiry', in *Zhizn' v kino: Veterany o sebe i svoikh tovarishchakh*, Moscow, 1971, pp.232–247.

Medvedkin, Alexander, 'Kinofel'etony', in *Iz istorii kino: dokumenty i materialy*, Moscow, 1974, pp.61–86.

Medvedkin, Alexander '294 dnia na kolesakh', in *Iz istorii kino: dokumenty i materialy*, Moscow, 1977, pp.32–57.

Medvedkin, Alexander, 'Chto takoe kinopoezd', in *Iz istorii kino: dokumenty i materialy*, Moscow, 1985, pp.27–62.

Medvedkin, Aleksandr, '*Okaiannaia sila*: russkaia narodnaia skazka', *Kinovedcheskie zapiski*, no. 57, pp.183–214.

Publications about Medvedkin in English and other languages

Eisenschitz, Bernard (ed.), *Lignes d'ombre: une autre histoire du cinéma soviétique (1926–1968)*, Milan, 2000.

Eisenstein, Sergei, 'Happiness', in *Sergei Eisenstein: Selected Works*, vol. 3: *Writings 1934–1947*, Richard Taylor (ed.), London, 1996, pp.52–55.

Leyda, Jay, 'Une autre résurrection', *Ecran*, February 1972, pp.51–52.

Leyda, Jay, *Kino: A History of Russian and Soviet Film*, London, 1960.

Marcel, Martin, 'Propos d'Alexandre Medvedkine: receuillis au magnétophone à Moscou', *Ecran*, February 1972, pp.46–48.

Taylor, Richard, 'Interview with Alexander Medvedkin', in *Inside the Film Factory: New Approaches to Russian and Soviet Cinema*, Richard Taylor and Ian Christie (eds.) London, 1991, pp.165–175.

Walsh, Martin, 'The Political Joke in "Happiness"', *Screen*, 19:1, Spring 1978, pp.79–89.